How to Beat
the
Energy Thieves®
And Make Your Life Better!

Book 1

How To Take Your Energy Back From Alcohol, Drugs, Tobacco, Bullying, Stealing, Gambling, Gangs, Knives and Guns And Find Your True Path In Life

Jess Miller

'How well you manage the energy you are determines for the most part how life on earth will be for you.'

How to Beat the Energy Thieves® And Make Your Life Better - Book 1
Alcohol, Drugs, Tobacco, Bullying, Stealing, Gambling, Gangs, Knives, Guns.

© MillerBooks 2010   First published in 2010 by MillerBooks   ISBN: 978-0-9565831-0-9
Cover: Jess & MarcellinoDesign.com

Jess's other titles:

How to Beat the Energy Thieves® And Make Your Life Better - Book 2
Emotions, Food, People, Major Problems, Traumas, Winning.

© MillerBooks 2010   First published in 2010 by MillerBooks   ISBN: 978-0-9565831-1-6

How to stop emotions such as fear, loneliness, anger or hatred holding your energy hostage.
How to resist turning food into an energy thief.
How to get the better of people who are acting as energy thieves against you.
How to beat exam or public speaking nerves.
How to cope with financial wipe-out.
How to beat the energy thieves that live in your past and hurt you in the present.
Unique and powerful insights to help you protect your energy and find your way to a better life.

How to Beat the Energy Thieves® And Make Your Life Better - Book 3
Education, Indoctrination, The Media, Technology, Role Models, Gossip, Trivia, Self Importance and Arrogance

© MillerBooks 2010   **To be published in 2012** by MillerBooks   ISBN: 978-0-9565831-4-7

How your life teachers may not be teaching you the best way to live out your existence.
How your training by the system we live under enables it to control your energy.
How the media influences your opinions about life and the way you live it.
How technology can be a energy thief unless you use it only for what you absolutely need.
How role models can dramatically affect the direction of your life.
How idle gossip can ruin your life and the lives of others.
How the trivia of life can consistently bog down your energy.
How self importance and arrogance can steal away the energy that belongs to you.

We're All In This Together
Help Through Stressful and Depressive Times
© 2000 Jester Publications & 2010 MillerBooks   ISBN: 978-0-9565831-2-3

Explaining the journey we travel down into and back from depression and giving twelve simple, but powerful and proven self-help therapies that anyone can use to make themselves feel better in stressful or depressive times.

The Great Convergence
© 2000 Jester Publications & 2010 MillerBooks   ISBN: 978-0-9565831-3-0

A light-hearted, humorous tale recounting strange encounters, even stranger goings on, scheming, greed, deceit, hilarity, chaos and triumph that occur when thousands of people unexpectedly converge upon a simple English village auction.

I wrote this book for You

Individual sections of this book may not make sense on their own. Only if you read the book from the beginning will you fully understand how to beat the energy thieves operating against you or someone you know.

1	A New Beginning	1
2	Understanding Energy	3

	The System	5
	The Great Reactionary	7
	Honesty	8
	The Question	8
	Good and Evil	9
	The Passing of Time	10

3	Alcohol	13

	The Alcohol Exercise	14
	Alcohol and Evil	19
	The Henchman	21
	The Energy Thief Alcohol	22
	The Hangover	25
	Get Real!	34
	How You Can Win!	36
	Do Not Engage!	39
	The Greatest Weapon of All	41
	Helping Others	44
	The Counter Attack!	47

4	Drugs	51

	Dependency	54
	The Energy Thief Drugs	59
	The Slave Trade	61

5	Tobacco	63

	The Energy Thief Tobacco	65

6   Bullying   70

        Change Yourself   79

7   Stealing   80

8   Gambling   84

9   Gangs   90

        The Gang   95
        Gang Busters   96

10 Knives, Guns, Weapons   100

11 Your Circumstances   107

12 Where's The Thief?   111

13 The Garden of Energy Thieves   114

14 Managing Your Energy   119

15 50 Ways To Help Someone   123

I used to hold a licence to sell alcohol, I've consumed my fair share of it and for a long time I was tricked into thinking that drinking alcohol was compulsory, that it was important for me to drink it.

Today I am an alcohol-free zone and I use alcohol as one of the great examples of an energy thief.

I **never** tell people **not** to drink alcohol, **not** to take drugs or **not** to smoke tobacco because it's their energy to do with as they wish.

I simply help those who have become the fallout from these three industries and the system we live under to understand what is really happening to their energy when they innocently reach out to energy thieves such as alcohol, drugs and tobacco.

I do not have system trained medical or therapist qualifications.
I employ the experience gained from my lifetime's journey of learning to help as many of my fellow human beings as I can who are finding their journey difficult.

Once you become fully aware of your potential destruction by many of the things you innocently reach out to you will become determined to stop them stealing your energy and making your life miserable, often without you having realised that it was they who were responsible.

The power to do this is within you, it simply needs accessing and unleashing.

Gaining knowledge and wisdom makes your life journey easier, but it is impossible for any of us to know everything we need to about life so that we can protect ourselves against the many energy thieves out there that are determined to do us serious harm.

I hope that within the pages of this book you will find a great deal you can use to protect the precious gift of energy you have received and that you can pass on to your friends so they can protect their energy in the same way.

Jess Miller

Finding and Following Your True Path is Positive

Diversion From Your True Path is Negative

Good = Light = Positive

Evil = Dark = Negative

Positive gives you energy

Negative steals your energy

A New Beginning

A part of Africa is suffering a severe, long lasting drought.

Everything is dying and it has been like this for months.

The grasses and vegetation are withered and burnt and the streams and rivers have disappeared, forcing everything that lives into a desperate search for water.

Now even the elephants with all their ancient knowledge handed down for generations cannot find water in the old sources under the dry river beds.

The heat is interminable and the temperature falls but little during the nights whilst the ground still burns underfoot.

Everywhere is quiet. No joyful songs of nature can be heard as the existence of birds, fish, animals and human beings ends.

It is a sombre scene as day after day whatever still lives clings desperately to life by the merest thread as hope dwindles.

One day, after several months of searing heat, a tiny droplet of water falls from the heavens only to evaporate high in the atmosphere.

A short while later a few more droplets attempt to reach the ground, but fail.

After some hours, as high cloud begins to move in slowly, a single droplet makes it to the ground and evaporates upon contact, then another follows, then another.

A few hours later light rain is falling.

Those elephants still alive stand waiting patiently.

They know what is finally coming as the rain gradually increases.

Soon a powerful African storm has arrived as torrential rain roars down upon the land.

Remaining life forms creep from their hiding places to drink from puddles.

Within a day of lashing rain the streams begin to gently flow and the rivers slowly begin their journey once more.

Within three days and nights of torrential rain life has begun again.

Lakes fill, fish swim, birds fly, vegetation resumes its growth and animals and humans can flourish once again.

Water, the life saver and bringer of the energy essential to the existence of life on earth, has finally arrived

And all living creatures so dependent upon its lifeline can begin to regain their tenuous foothold upon the surface of our planet once more.

<u>Understanding Energy</u>

Water is the energy that is life on earth.

Without the energy of water nothing lives, including you and me.

You are comprised of around 75% water –

Therefore you are energy!

But along with your great gift of energy came a question:

How will you manage this great gift of your energy?

Will you manage it well?

Will you manage it badly?

Or will you simply hand the management of the greatest gift in the universe over to someone or something else?

It is you who determines what will happen in your life through deciding:

What you <u>will</u> give your energy to

What you <u>won't</u> give your energy to

By doing so you determine for the greater part how your life will be.

Unfortunately there are many tempting things to reach out to in our world that:

Look exciting

Appear to be your friends

Hold out the promise of comfort

Guarantee they'll make you feel better

In reality their only intention is to steal all of your energy away from you if you give them half a chance.

These are the Energy Thieves

The energy thieves have but one objective, to tear your life apart and stop you accessing and using your true powers to find and follow your true path and live out your true purpose as a happy, fulfilled and content human being filled with good purpose and living a beneficial existence for you and those around you.

The energy thieves are determined to stop you using your energy to do good while you are here.

They are determined to stop you accessing the all important true powers that lie within you because through using these powers you really can make a difference for the better to your life and to our world.

Always think of yourself as the centre of the greatest gift in the universe, the energy that has been given to you, and be constantly aware of the multitude of energy thieves out there in our world who will never stop trying to steal your great gift of energy in order to do you serious damage and knock your life off course.

The System

The system of life we live under involves everything that you get knowledge from, that teaches and trains and indoctrinates the energy and intelligence you are from the moment you arrive here.

The system cares little about you it cares only about continuing to exist in its present form, so it keeps forever binding the energy given to humanity, including the energy given to you, to itself.

It does this by making sure that when you first arrive and begin crying out for knowledge it gives you only the knowledge it requires you to have in its attempts to ensure that your energy will serve it for all of your life.

Knowledge is power
Withholding knowledge is power too

If the system gives you only the limited knowledge it wants you to have then it has power over you through its limitation of your knowledge and the consequent way it has been able to ensure you only have that limited knowledge with which to manage your energy and live out your life.

The biggest way the system 'gives' you knowledge about life is to force you to have to seek most of it out for yourself as you fight your way through the daily jungle of experiences it throws at you.

You are forced to try and guide the energy you are safely through a daily minefield of energy thieves if you want to ensure that you put your great gift of energy to good use while you are here.

By going through this multitude of life experiences you may (or you may not) gain proper perspective over the system we live under.

If you do gain proper perspective you will understand that instead of letting the system dictate how you are going to use your energy and how you will be while you are here it is better to live alongside the system, using it only for what you absolutely need and not letting it dictate your existence to you, which it has no right to do.

Do not simply be a servant of the system, be an improver of it

To do this you will need to keep your mind and heart open to being receptive to learning new things at all times.

**Two of the greatest callings for the human spirit
are learning and helping other people**

Down this road lies your understanding that the system we live under isn't everything and that by making sure it is you who is guiding and managing the energy you are and not something else that is doing so you can do great and positive things in our world whilst you are here.

By helping more and more people you will be able to find your true path in life which will lead to your true purpose and if you can live out your true purpose you will become a happier, more fulfilled and contented human being filled with good purpose and living a beneficial experience both for yourself, those around you and those you have yet to meet.

You can make a truly big difference for the better in our world by helping other people in whatever way you are able to and so drive the energy you have been given down the road of good.

By improving the life of others you will improve your own life

And by living in this way you will consistently beat the system by taking the management of your energy, the energy that belongs to you, back into your own hands.

The Great Reactionary

The system teaches you everything you know and it needs you to react to every event that happens in your life without thinking so that it can control your energy.

Look before you leap!

If you don't take a step back and think about what is happening before you react to events then the management of the energy that has been given to you is easy for the system we live under to control.

The more you learn and understand about life the bigger your comfort zone becomes and the less you will react without thinking.

The less you learn and understand about life the smaller your comfort zone will remain and the more you will make the mistake of instantly reacting to and consequently being hurt by all kinds of things that happen in your life.

When a small comfort zone is pricked it takes a major hit

When a large comfort zone is pricked it is hardly affected

Learning everything you can about yourself and about life is one of the great keys to an existence where your energy will be truly managed by you and not by something else.

Honesty

Honesty is a hugely powerful way to make your life better.

The greatest basis for a relationship between two human beings is mutual honesty, it is one of the strongest foundations to build a lasting relationship upon.

Being honest with yourself about your life at all times will be of enormous benefit to you on your journey, whereas kidding or lying to yourself about your life will turn it into an empty shell and ensure it becomes a harder and harder road for you to travel, a road that can easily lead you to despondency, delusion, dependency, desolation and depression.

The Question

Asking yourself the following question **twice** every day looking into a mirror in complete honesty with yourself will gradually help to rid you of the dangers of kidding yourself about your life and stop you living any kind of a lie.

Though you may feel awkward about doing this at first in time you will find amazing answers coming from deep within you that will help you move your life forward and enable you to find your true path:

**In the moment my journey of life on earth is over
what do I want to be able to say
my life has been about?**

Good and Evil

Good and evil are ever present light and dark energies that swirl around you every moment of your life. The never ending war that rages between them and the intense battles they fight every second of your existence are being fought over the greatest of all prizes:

The energy that belongs to you!

Always remember that good works mysteriously, but that evil works deviously.

So you better quickly start working out how deviously evil might be working against you in its attempts to steal your energy before it succeeds.

There are only two paths you can direct your energy down in this world, the path of good or the path of evil.

It's up to you which one you follow.

If you follow the path of evil it will very soon end up owning all of the energy that was given to you – forever.

If you mess with evil, evil will mess with you!

This means the further down the dark road you travel the harder it will be for you to get back onto the road of good until soon evil will own the energy that was given to you for all eternity and your opportunity of returning to the path of good will have vanished forever.

You will hardly notice yourself slipping down the dark road because evil makes itself so deviously easy to follow.

On the other hand following the road of good is the ultimate test of how tough you really are deep down inside and how competent you become at managing the great gift of energy you have received so that you can negotiate your way safely through the daily minefield of energy thieves and make a difference for the better in our world whilst you are here.

The Passing of Time

It seems as if you will live forever, **you won't.**

It seems as if nothing can harm you, **it can.**

It seems as if you are invincible, **you are not.**

You think that nothing bad will ever happen to you, **it will.**

It feels as if you are the only one with problems, **you are not.**

It seems as if everyone else has it easy, **they do not.**

You think you are important, **you are, but not in any way that the system has been teaching or kidding you.**

You have only this tiny fragment of time in which to make the very best use of the energy you have been given, for in what will seem like a flash your brief moment of life here on earth will be over.

So it's up to you...

**Unless you believe in reincarnation
your life is not a dress rehearsal!**

It is time to understand that you have received the greatest gift in the universe and that out there in our world are countless devious and extremely dangerous energy thieves who will never give up trying to steal your great gift of energy so they can divert you from your true path and destroy your life and your existence...

How to Beat
The
Energy Thieves®

Alcohol, Drugs & Tobacco

The Three Horsemen of <u>Your</u> Apocalypse?

Alcohol

Always think of yourself as the centre of your energy and that out there in our world are countless cunning, devious and dangerous energy thieves determined to steal your energy so they can destroy your life. Most energy thieves have no energy, no life force and no power until you give them some of yours and then they'll steal it all!

The Alcohol Exercise:

Important: Before reading further please half fill a bottle with something to represent alcohol and place it in front of you.

Please do this now, before continuing, then you will be ready.

You are going to **PRETEND** to pick the bottle up and drink from it, so put it just out of your reach.

But **KEEP LOOKING** at the liquid in the bottle **and never take your eyes from it,** a little difficult whilst reading, but keep looking at it as much as you can or get a friend to read this to you so you can keep your eyes on the liquid in the bottle and gain full benefit from this exercise.

Please do the following exercise **very, very slowly,** **PRETENDING** to reach out and drink from the bottle.

The three lines in each paragraph refer to:

You
Your Energy
The Liquid in the Bottle

Take this slowly and think deeply about what is happening:

The Alcohol Exercise

You
Your Energy
The Liquid in the Bottle

Lift Your Hand
Energy Begins To Leave You
Now It Stirs From Its Powerless State

Slowly Begin To Reach Out
Energy Is Leaving You
Now It's Awake!

Extend Your Arm
Energy Is Pouring Out Of You
Now It's Cheering!

Grip The Bottle
You Are Suffering A Massive Energy Loss!
Now It's Laughing At You!

Lift The Bottle And Hold It In Front Of You
50% Of Your Energy Has Already Left You!
It Has Gained 50% Of Your Energy!

Open The Bottle
Your Energy Is Fading
It Is So Happy Because It Knows What Is Coming!

Put The Bottle To Your Lips
Get Ready To Say Goodbye To Your Energy!
The Liquid In The Bottle Is About To Be Fully Energised!

Take A Drink….
You Have Lost Your Energy To The Liquid In The Bottle!
It's Mission To Steal Your Energy Is Complete!

STOP DRINKING!
The Energy Flow Goes Into Reverse!
Now It Screams In Fear!

Extend Your Arm And Hold The Bottle Above The Table
Your Energy Comes Flooding Back To You!
It's Suffering Blind Terror!

Put The Bottle Down But Keep Hold Of It
50% Of Your Energy Has Already Returned!
It's Howling In Pain Because Your Energy Is Leaving It!

Let Go Of The Bottle
100% Of Your Energy Has Returned!
You Have Devastated The Liquid In The Bottle!

Return Your Hand
Your Energy Belongs To You Once More!
It Has Lost The Battle Over Your Energy!

You have been created as Energy, LifeForce and Power

The Liquid in The Bottle has
No Energy, No LifeForce and No Power

Until you give it some of yours!

And then it will steal it all - if it can!

What just happened?

You reached out with the energy that belongs to you and energised the liquid in the bottle and by managing your energy in this way you allowed the liquid in the bottle to get inside your body, inside the sacred vessel you have been given to sail through this extraordinary journey of life within. Only once it gets there does it have the opportunity to begin stealing your energy and doing you harm, or stealing a lot of your energy and doing you really serious damage, or stealing all of your energy away from you and ending your existence.

The body you have been given needs to be treated with the utmost respect and maintained at the optimum level at all times for all of your life. It needs the right fuel, exercise and rest and it needs to be kept stress free. Imagine if you were to put the wrong kind of fuel in your car or not maintain it properly what would happen.

Your body is exactly the same with one big exception –
you can always buy another car!

In the moment you reached out and gave the energy that is yours to the liquid in the bottle (that had no energy before you reached out to it) and let it trick you into putting it inside yourself, you gave it the opportunity to steal 100% of your energy from you.

You gave away the energy that belongs to you
The Greatest Gift in the Universe
to a liquid in a bottle

It gained the ability to take your energy away from you only after you had given your energy to it first.

Not only that, but after you let go of the bottle you **thought** you had taken 100% of your energy back, but once you had placed the alcohol inside your body you had already begun losing your energy to it. So you didn't take all of your energy back, it only felt as if you did, and if you were to keep putting more alcohol inside yourself you would keep losing more and more of your energy to it.

You have just been introduced to an energy thief!

It was you who energised the liquid in the bottle and it was you who gave it the chance to steal away the very energy that you are.

Look at the liquid in the bottle.

What has it done since you put it there?

Absolutely nothing!

Why?

Because it has no energy, no life force and no power!

You were created as all three!

Alcohol has absolutely no power whatsoever and don't ever let anyone tell you that it has.

If you think that alcohol is hugely powerful that's your system training kicking in to deliberately try and confuse you.

Alcohol has absolutely no power whatsoever!

Would you like to prove it?

Look at the liquid in the bottle…

If you were to fold your arms and sit and stare at it for the next one billion years it could not have damaged you.

It could not have enslaved the energy you are into the hell of alcoholism.

It could not have ended your existence.

Alcohol can do none of these things because it has no energy, no life force and no power.

Alcohol has to sit and wait for you to reach out with your energy and energise it and only then, once you have put it inside your body, can it set about doing you serious damage or even end your existence.

If you never reach out to alcohol with your energy it will have to sit where it is, powerless to harm you forever.

Only once you make the mistake of putting alcohol inside you can it gain your energy, your life force and your power by stealing it away from you, sometimes without your even realising it until it's too late.

This is the work of a 'henchman'.

A henchman is someone who does the dirty work for someone else.

Don't you think that the liquid in the bottle that can do you so much damage once it gets inside you might just be being used against you in order to divert you from following your true path and finding your true purpose?

And are you simply going to allow the greatest gift in the universe to be taken away from you so easily?

Are you simply going to wave a white flag and surrender the gift?

Alcohol and Evil

Alcohol, like many substances we human beings abuse, was put on the earth for our benefit.

Alcohol is used for specialised cleaning purposes in industry and it is alcohol that is swabbed on your skin before the doctor sticks a needle in you, because it kills bacteria.

Seems to me alcohol is a pretty good thing to have around.

Alcohol is not evil and saying that alcohol is evil is wrong!

The Puritans called alcohol evil, satan, the devil.

Just looking at the liquid in the bottle sitting there, powerless to do anything will tell you that it is none of these things.

Evil is evil, alcohol is alcohol.

Saying that alcohol is evil is just plain wrong.

And the people who work in the alcohol industry are not evil, they're people trying to get along and make a living the same as you are.

Whether they make alcohol, package it, transport it, sell it or serve it they are most definitely not evil people (although there could be one or two evil ones amongst them as there are everywhere!).

Working in the alcohol industry does not make them evil.

The problem begins once alcohol has been distilled into consumable form because right there and then evil is provided with **the opportunity to hijack it,** turn it into its henchman and use it against you if it can for the incredibly evil purpose of stealing the very energy you have been given away from you and knocking your life off course.

Always remember that it will be you and you alone who will determine the future of alcohol in your life through the way in which you manage the great gift of energy you have received.

Only you can determine this, no one can determine it for you.

It is you who decides what you will reach out to and what you will not reach out to in life.

The Henchman

As evil begins to use alcohol against you it first chooses which particular henchman it wants to trap your energy with.

All of its henchmen must be dressed in attractive packages and have distinctive labels so that you can instantly recognise the one you want to surrender your energy to.

The liquid in the bottle must also have a certain colour, aroma and taste that you will find overwhelmingly appealing.

Evil will then use unwitting agents to encourage you to put its henchman inside your body by saying things to you like:

'Go on, have a drink!'

'It'll do you good!'

'Try some of this!'

'What can I get you?'

'Would you like another one?'

'You've given up alcohol? How do you have any fun?'

'You've given up alcohol? You're not welcome here!'

This is how evil sets its trap to trick you into giving away the energy that belongs to you to its henchman.

Maybe the henchman will take just a little of your energy at first, then a little bit more and a little bit more until finally, precious drop by precious drop, the henchman will have stolen all of your energy from you.

The Energy Thief Alcohol

When a thief breaks into your home and stands in your holy of holies pointing his flashlight around and his mouth drops open at the sight of all your worldly treasures, the piles of gold and silver bars, the platinum ingots, the trunks brimming over with cash, the countless boxes filled with diamonds and priceless jewellery, the paintings by Monet and Van Gogh and the drawers full of fabulous Swiss watches (that's right, he's in your place!) - does he look around and say,

'Well, if it's alright with you I'll just take this glass ornament?'

Does he heck!

Within 15 minutes his pal has a truck backed up to your home and when you return from holiday there isn't even a light fitting, a light switch or a door handle left.

If you're lucky they might have left you the doors!

A thief will take everything from you that it can and the great energy thief alcohol is no different!

Evil knows that if it can hijack alcohol and get you to make the mistake of reaching out to it with the energy that you are and put it inside your body then it can do you really serious harm, it can even steal all of your energy away from you and kill you, which is its **ultimate aim.**

If it can't achieve this immediately it will do so in a while and in the meantime it will try to imprison the energy that you are within its hell of alcoholism. The very least that it wants is to make sure that your energy spirals ever downwards through the life of an alcoholic, however long or short a life that may be.

Evil knows that if you have the wrong genes, the wrong DNA or the wrong metabolism (in its eyes the right ones) it can use alcohol against you to deadly effect because it knows you are vulnerable to the attack of its henchman.

It wants nothing more than to damage the energy you are and get your energy **'off planet'** before you have a chance to find and follow your true path to your true purpose.

You are at war with evil and you don't even know it!

And that, my friend, is most definitely not your fault.

It's the fault of the system we live under that never wants you to hear the message I'm passing to you now, which is a measure of how important this message is.

Oh, I know what you're thinking…

'But Jess, I feel better when I have a drink.'

No, you don't!

You never feel 'better' when you drink alcohol it's just that the henchman has tricked you into thinking you do.

Let's agree that you definitely feel something when you drink alcohol.

It's the word 'better' we disagree on.

If you think you feel 'better' then you have either never known how to feel better or you've forgotten how.

Here's a scenario you might be familiar with:

Your day has been a total nightmare from the moment you got up. Everything has gone wrong. You've argued with your family, friends and work colleagues. Your day's work has been nothing short of a catastrophe and you haven't had a second to catch your breath. Your job is under threat. You're in debt and running out of options and your partner has threatened to leave unless you sort it out. Your best friend just passed away. You got a speeding ticket on the way home after which your car broke down and you had to walk three miles back to your house in the pouring rain without a coat or umbrella.

Finally you arrive back at your place soaking wet and miserable and, as you walk through the front door and cross the threshold, **you need a drink.**

Sound familiar?

So you head for where you keep it and open the door to your stash.

And there it is, the old familiar, your 'friend', the one you know will 'help' you and is going to make you feel 'better'.

You find the sight of the bottle, the weight and feel of it in your hand and the colours of the label and the liquid inside comforting and reassuring.

And you are absolutely positive that you are in total control of your energy and what you are doing.

But nothing could be further from the truth!

As you undo the bottle the aroma of your favourite alcohol fills you with anticipation and you pour yourself a large one and take a big drink of it, then another and another.

In a while you pour yourself another large one as the thief cunningly begins its devious work upon you.

Your muscles begin to relax.

The tension in you begins to ease.

You begin to feel **'better'**…

Really?

Is that what you honestly think is happening?

In that case I'll come back to you in a little while.....

The Hangover

Have you ever experienced a hangover?

How did you feel?

Lousy?
Awful?
Terrible?
Nauseous?
Did you have a headache?
Did you feel like hell?

Now that's strange, you felt like hell?

Isn't hell where the devil lives?

And yet you felt like hell right in the very core of your being?

But surely heaven is up there and hell is down below like the system teaches us?

Yet you felt like hell right inside your body, inside the sacred vessel you have been given to journey through this incredible experience of life within.

That is worth thinking about very, very carefully my friend.

I have the distinct feeling that when you felt like hell during your hangover – evil was really close to you at that time.

Did you ever have a hangover that was so bad you wished you were dead?

During your hangover did you have much energy?

No?

Of course you didn't!

You had put so much of the thief inside yourself that it was able to steal almost all of the energy that you are away from you!

Do you realise how lucky you have been to survive one single hangover, never mind multiple hangovers?

Do you understand that when the thief ran its deviousness upon you it resulted in your having so little energy left you couldn't think properly, talk properly or walk properly because virtually all of your energy had been stolen from you, which is why you weren't capable of doing even these simple things?

When you woke up face down the next morning on your bed or in the same chair you had consumed the thief in the night before and wondered where the heck you were and how you got there do you understand how lucky you were that you had not choked on your own vomit as your body desperately tried to get rid of what it now regarded as 'poison' because you had remorselessly kept pouring more and more of the thief into your body, but it no longer had enough energy left to be able to clear it from you?

The sacred vessel that you need to preserve at all times in the best possible condition so that you can continue your journey of life within it was screaming a stark warning at you to stop consuming more of the thief.

But did you take any notice of that warning?

No.

So the henchman was easily able to continue carrying out its devious work upon you.

But it's cool to get drunk, isn't it?

It's great to be able to 'run away' from the problems the system throws at you and immerse yourself in alcoholic oblivion, isn't it?

It's nice not to be able to feel any of life's pain or loneliness anymore, isn't it?

But I guarantee that the very same problems, pain and loneliness will still be there tomorrow.

You may not be

Do you realise that when you were in this state, full of the thief and stripped of your energy, how lucky you were that you didn't stagger out to your vehicle (because the thief had stolen so much of your energy you could no longer walk properly), somehow manage to unlock it, start it up, drive off and kill yourself and a whole bunch of innocent human beings as well?

Do you understand how lucky you have been to survive one single hangover and still be here, never mind multiple hangovers?

How about the luck you've had that you haven't suffered alcohol poisoning and one of your major organs such as your liver hasn't packed up?

Do you think when evil's henchman was encouraging you to go all the way to the point of your hangover he might also have cunningly and deviously been getting you to do some serious damage to your liver?

Don't you understand you need your liver in 100% good condition to be able to continue your existence?

Look at the liquid in the bottle....

What has it done since you put it there?

Absolutely nothing!

And you know why it has done nothing, don't you?

Now let's go back to the way alcohol makes you feel 'better' and the scenario I was outlining before.

The tension in you has eased and you've poured yourself a third drink.

You are now deep under the influence of the thief!

Evil has been successful in convincing you that alcohol is actually helping you, when nothing could be further from the truth.

That feeling of 'better' when you put the thief inside you is nothing more than a smokescreen to blind you from its real intention.

What you are actually feeling are the first lulling, coaxing, beckoning, enticing sensations as the henchman's devious plan to steal your energy away from you gets underway.

The thief is saying to you **'hey, have some of me, I'll make you feel good, I'll ease your pain – I'll make you feel better!'**

You are now managing your energy so badly by directing it down the dark road the thief wants you to travel instead of the true path you should be following if you want to get to that better life.

You are being conned, suckered into believing that you are feeling 'better' and that **the more of the thief you drink the 'better' you are going to feel...**

Wrong!

All energy thieves are <u>Con Artists</u>!

And the con that every energy thief runs is to get you to think that:

<u>You</u> are in control of <u>It</u>

When all the time

<u>It</u> is in control of <u>You</u>!

And all the time it is in control of you the henchman is luring you down the dark road that leads to your hangover.

From the moment those first easing sensations ran through your body you were losing energy to the thief and the more alcohol you drank and the more those 'feeling better' sensations grew within you the more energy was pouring out of you until you had lost every last ounce of it and the con run by the energy thief alcohol was complete.

And all of this happened because when you came home after a bad day you **needed** a drink.

It's the word **'need'** that tells the real story behind most energy thieves.

If you ever <u>need</u> to drink alcohol you're an alcoholic
meaning -you haven't got it, it's got you!

If you <u>cannot live</u> without drinking alcohol for an hour, a day, a week, a month, a year or the rest of your life – you are dependent upon alcohol and you're an alcoholic.

There is no better definition than that demonstrated by the word **'need'**.

If you **need** to drink alcohol you are addicted to it, the con that has been run on you is complete and the great energy thief alcohol already owns the energy that used to belong to you.

You've given your energy away to the thief and you think that <u>You</u> are running <u>It</u>.

But because of the very fact that You <u>need</u> It

<u>It</u> is running <u>You</u>

This is the con, pure and simple.

Alcohol is running you and stealing your energy through your dependency upon it.

There's no other valid definition of an alcoholic, if you think there is then with respect you're kidding yourself and remember what happens if you kid (lie) to yourself about your life, it will quickly turn into an empty shell and you will become an extremely unhappy human being.

You do not feel __better__ when you drink alcohol!

You feel __different__!

You are simply being conned down the dark road the thief wants you to follow, the diversion of your energy away from your true path.

There are countless things you can do to make yourself feel better that do not involve consuming alcohol, here is a __very__ short list of some of them:

Get a massage.
Work out.
Go cycling.
Go sailing.
Go rambling.
Go motor racing.
Enjoy your hobby.
Enjoy a swim.
Enjoy a sauna.
Enjoy a jacuzzi.
Make some fresh fruit and vegetable juice and give your body the vitamins and minerals it needs.
Take your dog for a walk and a romp.
Go sit in a wood and listen to the wind in the trees and relax.
Walk in the rain and enjoy the power of the energy bringer.
Walk on a beach.
Put on some relaxing music.
Light your favourite incense and cook yourself a nice fresh meal.
Take a long relaxing shower or bath.
Spend a while meditating and relaxing.
Go and see a friend and have a laugh and a chat about how you both feel and help each other work out your life problems.
Go see a movie.
Go to the theatre.

Make love.....
Make love again.....
Make love again.....

There is so much you can do to make yourself feel better and by feeling better through taking good care of yourself and your body in these ways you will not only be retaining energy, **you will be gaining energy!**

Following the road the thief will lead you down ensures you will lose the energy you have been given.

Stop lying to yourself that alcohol makes you feel 'better', it does not, it makes you feel **different**, this is the con of evil's henchman tricking you into surrendering your energy.

Is evil winning in your life?

If so.........why are you letting it?

Alcohol cannot enter your body and do you harm if you don't reach out to it and give it your energy in the first place.

Alcohol cannot pick itself up, pour itself into a glass and pour itself into you, it needs you to mismanage the energy you are by reaching out to it to give it your energy before it can get inside you.

If you never make the mistake of reaching out to it, misguidedly thinking it's some kind of friend who is going to help you, which it never is and never will be, it will have to sit where it is forever, completely powerless to harm you while you go about enjoying your life by putting your increasing energy to good use.

Do you know someone whose existence was ended early from alcohol related causes?

If you don't you're pretty unique.

I have known many people who were robbed of their energy by alcohol well before their time, a number in their teens, some in their twenties, some in their thirties, some in their forties and so on.

Alcohol took all of their energy away from them.

Their existence was ended through alcohol related car crashes, choking on their own vomit, liver problems, alcohol induced cancer, etc.

In their case evil won, they are no longer here to have the opportunity that you do to try to find your true path and purpose.

They no longer have the opportunity that you do of doing something good with your energy whilst you are here.

This was the opportunity evil wanted to stop them having!

Just read those last two sentences again.

I've seen people in the grip of the thief, as I have been myself, drinking in pubs day after day when there is so much more they could have been doing with their energy in the tiny fragment of time they have here upon the earth.

They could have been using that time so constructively in making their lives happier, more enjoyable and more fulfilled in order to benefit themselves and everyone around them.

Their premature passing is both a great sadness and a massive endightment of the system we live under.

Do you think any of those people knew they should be looking in the mirror twice every day and asking themselves **the question** that in the moment their journey of life on earth was over what did they want to be able to say their lives had been about?

I don't think so.

I don't think anyone ever told them about **the question.**

What was it that they actually managed to do with the greatest gift in the universe?

Drink more alcohol than anyone else?

Didn't the system we live under bother to warn them about the thief or show them what their great gift of energy was really about and the war that was raging over it between good and evil?

Is that honestly what you would like to say your life has been about?

That you drank more alcohol than anyone else?

That's what you want to say you did with the greatest gift in the universe?

Do you honestly think that's all there is to do while you're here?

If so the system has done an appallingly good job on you.

One of the reasons why evil wants people to drink too much alcohol is because while they are drinking alcohol they are not using their energy to do good, because evil knows that if everyone who drinks alcohol were instead to use their energy doing good that would be a gigantic amount of good being done in our world.

If we took all the time and energy every human being expends on drinking alcohol and got them to use it to do good upon the earth how much good do you think that would be?

And if that amount of good was being done evil might just start losing the war against good, might it not?

So how successful at stopping good do you think evil is being in our world by using alcohol against so many of us?

Evil hijacks alcohol and uses it as an energy thief to push us into a dark downward spiral, not to take just a little of our energy away from us, but to take all of it if it can, leaving us with none.

Get Real!

Consuming alcohol can lead you to malnutrition, high blood pressure, lowered resistance to infections, increased risk of cancers of your mouth and throat, irreversible damage to your brain, your nervous system and severe damage to your heart, lungs, pancreas and liver and result in cirrhosis of your liver (if you don't know what this is you better look it up right now).

In Britain around **60,000** people die each year from alcohol related causes.

In the United States around **100,000** people die from alcohol related illnesses and accidents each year broken down as follows:

5% of deaths from diseases of the circulatory system
15% of deaths from diseases of the respiratory system
30% of deaths from accidents caused by fire
30% of accidental deaths by drowning
30% of suicides
40% of deaths due to accidental falls
45% of deaths in automobile accidents
60% of homicides

(Sources: NIDA Report, the Scientific American and Addiction Research Foundation of Ontario)

4,600,000 teenagers in the USA experience serious problems with alcohol.

There is no better time for evil's henchman to attack a human being than when it is young, when its energy is untainted and undamaged in order to find out whether that young human has the right genes, DNA or metabolism that it can get to work on.

And whenever you surrender the energy that is yours to alcohol, especially at a young age, you are giving evil's henchman the opportunity to end your life early.

Maybe it will end your life 5, 10, 20 or 30 years before your time.

Years you could have put to good use helping so many of the people around you.

Years you could have enjoyed with those you love and who love you.

Years in which you could have learned so much more about life and discovered you have the most incredible inner attributes and powers and used them to find your true path and purpose and become a much calmer, happier, fulfilled and beneficial human being whilst you were here.

Years in which you could have turned your life into something extra special, something you could have been proud to be able to say you achieved with the greatest gift in the universe.

But evil's henchman, the great energy thief alcohol, will steal all of your energy and deny you that opportunity by destroying you.

If you let it!

How You Can Win!

Some time ago I met a man in a recording studio where I was doing a voice over for one of my talks and we had an interesting conversation. After we had chatted for a while he suddenly said,

"Jess, I'm losing my wife and my family, I'm becoming an alcoholic. Every night when I get home I'm drinking three or four glasses of wine or more and falling asleep on the couch.
I don't know what is happening to me or why."

Someone saying this kind of thing to me right out of the blue happens all the time so I immediately started helping him get perspective on his problem and see what was really going on.

I asked if he had a bottle of alcohol and he found an empty bottle of beer. We put it on a table and I ran through the alcohol exercise you did earlier of pretending to drink from the bottle and described the energy flowing out of him to the liquid in the bottle.

Of course when I talk with somebody one on one the message I can pass to them is extremely powerful, not least because I can feel their energy changing and adjust what I'm saying accordingly.

I was feeling his energy changing, but he was still a little perplexed as he grappled with the problem until something incredible happened as I explained to him that he was at war with evil.

He was staring with great intensity at the empty bottle of beer as I talked and I felt a sudden massive shift within his energy.

This has happened many times when I'm helping people and we might call it 'the dawning of reality', a moment to treasure forever.

It was as if a light within him had suddenly been switched on.

Within a few minutes **he** was telling **me** all about alcohol and how **it** was attacking **him**, it was the most fantastic transformation of a human being to witness.

Some three months or so later he called me and said,

"Jess, I've stopped drinking alcohol and I've got my wife and my family and my life back! Do you know what I do?

I have a half empty bottle of wine on the sideboard in our lounge and every evening when I come home I ignore everyone in the house, it doesn't matter whether they are family, friends or strangers I go straight up to that bottle of alcohol and I shout at it at the top of my voice.....

I recognise you for who and what you are!

You are the Energy Thief that evil has sent to destroy my family and kill me!

Well you are not going to steal my Energy!

I am going to keep my Energy for me, for my family, for those I love and for those I want to help!

And you will never get any of it!

So you can go and rot in Hell!

And then I turn and hug everyone who is there and I take my wife and kids for a walk on the beach or we play in the park, or we go for a meal together or take in a movie and we are very, very happy.

I shout my declaration against alcohol in front of my kids and they are proud of me, even though they were a bit puzzled at first.

And you know the amazing thing?

Two of my friends have been there from time to time when I have done this and now they're both doing it and one of them who realised he had a problem has stopped drinking alcohol and the other has cut right down! Isn't this incredible?"

What was incredible was that he had rid himself of the thief that had been leading him down a darker and darker road.

I had simply handed him the key and he had cured himself through being bold enough to turn the key, open the door and step through onto a better path in life.

He had proved that anyone can win out over the energy thief alcohol.

And that includes you.

Do Not Engage

If you do not reach out and give your energy to alcohol it can never harm you!

If you don't engage your energy with alcohol you will make it far more difficult for evil to operate its energy thievery against you.

Energy thieves such as alcohol are a trap set to ensnare the energy that you are.

By the way, you didn't happen to be reading this thinking there would just be **one lone energy thief** out there, did you?

Sorry!

Dark energy operates through countless energy thieves on countless levels so you need to become fully aware of this minefield of energy thieves and keep directing your energy down the path of good so you can navigate your way safely through it and rid yourself of their threat!

You need to think of yourself as being the very centre of your energy and that out there in our world are countless energy thieves desperate to strip you of that energy and stop you finding your true path when only by finding your true path can you begin to make more and more sense of your life and how best to use the energy you have been given.

Thinking of yourself as the centre of your energy and asking yourself **the question** on page 8 twice every day will automatically help you change your life for the better.

In time you will begin to perceive and feel things you previously haven't been able to due to the massive loss of your energy to the energy thieves that was numbing your senses.

Gradually over time you will become stronger.

I don't mean the physical strength of the athlete, but you will find a quiet, determined strength growing within you.

You will become calmer as you work out how to follow the path of good and you will begin to enjoy managing and guiding the energy that you are in the best possible way, rather than having it managed for you and directed down the dark road by the energy thieves.

The Greatest Weapon of All

As I said before, you are at war with evil and you don't even know it, which is why you don't even recognise the battleground.

Evil recognises it all too well because the battleground where the fight is constantly raging over the energy that belongs to you is the very place where evil lives.

So where is this battleground?

In the moment, in the very instant that you see the great energy thief alcohol whether in a bottle, in a magazine, in a shop window, in a bar, in a mini bar in a hotel room, at someone's house, on TV, wherever you see it – in that very instant understand this:

You are already standing on the battleground and evil and its cohorts of darkness are coming straight at your heart to stop your life dead in its tracks!

And there you are, you poor, innocent, lonely, defenceless earth person having walked straight into its trap to find all of this evil bearing down upon you, coming to stamp out the very energy that you are.

Help!

Are you terrified of evil?

You don't have to be, it is not a requirement of your being here and it certainly isn't necessary.

If you have received the greatest gift in the universe do you honestly think it would have been given to you to leave you completely defenceless in the face of such an onslaught?

If it had been there wouldn't be any human beings left on our planet!

You most certainly have not been left defenceless because accompanying the greatest gift in the universe is the greatest weapon in the universe!

This is a weapon so enormously powerful that evil actually fears it!

That's right, evil actually fears it and that's why it has to attack you in its desperation to take you down and stop you finding out how to access the weapon and use it to defend your energy.

This phenomenal weapon was built into you at the moment of your creation for you to use to defend your energy against **all** of the energy thieves out there in life.

So in the instant you see the thief and realise you are standing on the battleground with evil and its cohorts of darkness charging straight at your heart here is how to activate the weapon that evil fears so much:

In the instant you see the thief immediately turn the energy that you are away from it and direct your energy towards helping someone!

Your lifetime's system training may well kick in to tell you this is nonsense, but as usual the reality is precisely the opposite, the system is trying to trick you into going back to the henchman.

By instantly taking charge of the energy that you are and directing it away from the thief towards helping someone else in whatever way you might be able to, in that very instant you will be defeating evil and its cohorts of darkness!

That's right, I'm talking about little old you – defeating evil!

If you do not engage with evil it cannot steal your energy!

It can try, but if you keep your energy permanently disengaged from evil and direct it towards helping other people you will be walking the path of good and evil will have the greatest difficulty in harming you directly by using energy thieves such as alcohol against you.

To turn selflessly and help another human being is the greatest calling for the human spirit!

This is the great weapon that has been placed within you, your ability to apply good and strong management to the energy that you are, and simply by accessing the weapon and employing really good management of your energy when confronted by the energy thief alcohol means that you have the ability to change your life for the better in a heartbeat.

When you turn to helping other people you will find the following things happening over time, as long as you keep helping people:

You will make real friends, not those so called friends you had when you were under the attack of the energy thieves and that you will find have now left you.

These new real friends will stand like rocks in your life to hang onto whilst the current of energy thieves swirls around you.

You will gain people's respect, the kind of respect that will mean people will want to talk to you and want to associate themselves with you.

You will find doors open to you that previously wouldn't have been and you must look for these doors opening.

Opportunities will come your way that previously wouldn't have and you must take these opportunities and journey onwards, don't let your comfort zone hold you back.

And slowly your life will get better and better, you will give and receive love, friendship, warmth, respect and help.

Your life will become more social on a very strong level of mutual support and you will become fulfilled, satisfied and much, much happier with your life.

Helping Others

Let me show you the nearest signpost to get your heart back and on the road...
If I can help you, if I can help you, if I can help you, just let me know...

'Hide in Your Shell' from 'Crime of the Century'
Roger Hodgson (Supertramp) 1974

You see the thief!
Direct your energy away from it!
Go help someone!

Imagine if you'd been helping people instead of all of the time in your life you've spent drinking too much alcohol!

Could you have helped a lot of people?

So what is so powerful about turning and helping someone else?

It's this - by helping someone else you are taking positive charge of your energy, instead of remaining reactive to the attack of the thief, and directing it down a different path, the path of good. By doing so you are giving new validation to your existence, you are giving it a real and proper value (not a false system value) and you have begun turning your life into a truly worthwhile experience.

And how do you help someone else when you're in a pretty desperate state yourself?

Any way you can!

Maybe it's a kind word, a smile, a chat, a phone call, visiting someone who is lonely and cheering them up, washing their dishes, walking their dog, giving advice to the best of your ability, helping someone paint their house, there are a million ways in which you can help other people, you just have to open your mind to finding them.
(You'll find 50 ways at the end of this book to start you off!)

And you may well be surprised to find there are a lot of people out there in our world who are having a much harder time than you.

Always remember that you need to give your help selflessly, not for reward, but from a deep desire within you to change your life for the better and after you have given your help simply walk away and say to yourself:

'Me! I did that! I'm in a bad place myself, but I helped a fellow human being and I feel better for having done so!'
Then go help someone else...
Then go help someone else...

This is the path of good and as you go about helping people in your own way things will begin to happen that will change your life for the better because you have changed the road you're on.

Now you are walking towards the Light.

You will be closing a door on the way you lived your life before, following the dark road, and whenever one door closes in life another door opens.

So stay alert, keep your eyes, your mind and your heart open, look for and recognise each door that is opening as you begin to change your life and make sure you stay bold, do not hang back when something, some opportunity to move your life forward suddenly appears through the help you have been giving others.

Grab that opportunity with both hands.

"When one door closes, another opens; but we often look so long and so regretfully upon the closed door that we do not see the one that has opened for us."
Alexander Graham Bell

It may not lead you to exactly what you were hoping for in life or what the system trained you to think you wanted in life, but as you step through each door that opens you will become more and more pleasantly surprised by the outcome.

You may have nothing right now and be at rock bottom, but you can still help other human beings and be proud of yourself for doing so, safe in the knowledge you have done something truly worthwhile with the greatest gift in the universe.

So the instant you see the thief, activate the weapon and never stop activating it:

Recognise the thief!

Remember what to do!

Activate the weapon!

Go help someone!

And here's a great question to start asking people:

How can I help?

Don't be surprised if occasionally you get a rude answer, always bear in mind that human beings are fickle and that you could well get your offer of help thrown back in your face.

Do not let this phase you, it's normal, rather let it spur you to move on to the next person to see how you can help them.

When I come across someone who is either aggressive or dismissive in their response to my offer of help I of course spend some time encouraging them that my offer is genuine, but if my reading of their energy is that I'm still facing a brick wall I move on to find someone who I really can help because my clock of life is ticking and I want to help as many people as possible in my remaining time here.

It's a bit like this book, some people will dismiss it, others will find it interesting and others will use its contents to help change their lives or the lives of their family or friends for the better.

You can't help all of the people all of the time, but you can still help one heck of a lot of people as you go through life.

The Counter Attack!

If you direct the energy that you are away from alcohol it is guaranteed that evil will launch a desperate all out counter attack to stop you.

You will feel an all-consuming, overwhelming, overpowering urge to go back to consuming alcohol.

But now you know this is the henchman at work, calling you to surrender the energy that you are to the thief again and you need to understand and accept that he will never stop calling you.

It's a battle you can always win
because it is you who controls the ultimate weapon!

Your instant good management of the energy you are!

If you come under this renewed attack know that it is one of evil's final assaults in its desperation to stop you taking your energy back to yourself.

So why would evil bother to launch such an assault upon you?

What the heck is it about you that causes evil to be so desperate to damage you?

Why would evil even bother to get out of bed and expend its energy upon little old you?

Because you are special and evil knows this only too well.

Being special does not in any way mean you are better than anyone else, thinking this would be foolishness created by your system training for no one human being is better than any other human being.

What it means is that you are special on a very specific level of sensitivity. This is not weakness, I'm talking about special abilities you have which you most probably don't realise because your system training has managed to block you from accessing them.

You have a special level of sensitivity that is the enemy of evil so evil has to attack you and knows it may well be able to successfully use energy thieves such as alcohol, drugs and tobacco against you.

But the genes, DNA and metabolism that it is hell bent on attacking have been given to you for an extremely important reason.

The reason you have received those genes, DNA and metabolism is so you are able to feel things that many people can no longer feel, especially those whose system indoctrination has locked their energy and their thought processes down into the whirlpool that is the system humanity lives under.

So you are special in this respect and you are charged with managing your energy and your special abilities in the very best possible way you can whilst you are here, because if you do you will be of the greatest benefit to humanity and our world in your own special way.

You definitely have attributes and abilities you are unaware of that have been blocked by your lifetime of system indoctrination and your loss of energy to the energy thieves.

The system we live under is designed to smother this sensitive ability and other hidden attributes and true powers within you, such as love and compassion, when you could be using them to find your true path and purpose.

**The system tells us that love and compassion
are weakness**

As usual the truth is completely the other way around

Love and Compassion are the True Powers upon the Earth!

As you begin to see through the smokescreen of system indoctrination that has been working against your inner abilities you can begin accessing these true powers through helping others and through encouraging the people you are helping to beat any energy thieves that may be damaging their lives.

But because you have had your energy diverted from your true path once before you could be at even more risk to energy thieves such as alcohol keeping on trying to divert you from it again and again, unless the changes you make to your life are permanent, which will require a fearless determination within you to find and follow your true path through helping others.

Well you didn't think evil wants to spend its time attacking those who are difficult to damage, did you?

It is just a fact of life that this is how it is for you, it is not a disaster because evil wants to damage you, it is absolute confirmation that you are special and that evil fears your abilities to do good upon the earth.

These special qualities and sensitivities are what evil is desperate to stop you accessing and using and it has its own devious ability to stop you, **but only if you let it.**

You have the ability to render evil useless by taking your energy back to yourself from the energy thieves and using it to help others and spread the knowledge of how they can do the same and so make their lives better.

This is what evil is desperate to stop you from doing!

For if it cannot take your energy from you then evil will be left with nothing and if you were to get others to understand about the energy thieves and encourage them to do something better with their energy, such as following the road of good by helping others, **evil would suddenly be losing the war against good over the energy that belongs to humanity!**

So when this counter attack in the form of the urge to consume alcohol comes over you in an effort to force you back to the thief, understand that you are under the last desperate attack of evil.

You are fighting to save the energy you are from destruction!

If you simply cave in and give up you will never be able to get back onto your true path nor ever find the true purpose of your life and you will have consigned the greatest gift in the universe to the wasteland of the energy thieves forever.

And remember:

The road to hell is paved with good intentions!

So don't just intend to beat the thief sometime in the future

Beat it now!

To seek out your true purpose and stay on your true path by taking your energy back from energy thieves such as alcohol so you can put it to good use means your life will begin to steadily change for the better and you will find yourself wanting to help others in your own way more and more as you move further down the road of good.

The energy that you are will grow as you nurture it in this way and you will grow and mature as a being.

You will become calmer and more fulfilled, wiser and more beneficial to those around you and you will live one heck of a lot longer because you will be suffering less stress.

The extension of your life that you are bringing about by managing the energy you are so wisely will give you time in which to build yourself into the most worthwhile being you can be whilst you are here.

By giving good, strong management to your energy:

You can beat the energy thief alcohol!

You are the Energy!

Don't Let The Energy Thieves Win!

Drugs

Always think of yourself as the centre of your energy and that out there in our world are countless cunning, devious and dangerous energy thieves determined to steal your energy so they can destroy your life. Most energy thieves have no energy, no life force and no power until you give them some of yours and then they'll steal it all!

Illegal drugs are the second of evil's three deadly henchmen and unlike alcohol, which is not evil yet can be hijacked by evil to use against you, drugs are the very embodiment of evil.

The difference between drugs and alcohol is that the people who make and sell alcohol do not do it with the deliberate intention of stealing the energy of the human being.

Those in the drugs trade do.

Unlike alcohol evil actually is the drug, the drug grower, the drug maker, the drug transporter and the drug dealer.

Pure evil runs through this chain, a chain of evil revolving around money, human misery and the theft and imprisonment of the great gift of human energy.

Nowhere else can the disaster that is the system we live under be seen more clearly than in the evil trade of illegal drugs.

Those who make drugs do so to make money.

Those who deliver drugs do so to make money.

Those who buy and sell drugs do so to make money.

Money is the root of all evil.

If you want to find evil at work just follow the trail of money as it climbs its way through the world of drugs and soon you will come across those who worship at the altar of the money-god and who, by doing so, create a life of misery for the hundreds of millions of people at the bottom of the drugs pyramid.

Those who try drugs may do so to experience adventure or experimentation or to run away from what is happening in their lives, lives they think they can 'escape' from with the 'help' of drugs.

In their mind taking drugs makes them feel 'better', exactly the same falseness as alcohol.

Those who indulge in drug use are seeking something extra in their lives, a different world to live in for a while to get away from their own inadequacy or the pain of everything that is wrong with their lives.

They are desperately seeking some kind of comfort, but fall foul of the con operated by the energy thief drugs by thinking it will help them and so the energy they are is conned into travelling down the wrong road.

Young people are usually introduced to drugs by a 'friend' and this is how the system perpetuates its stranglehold upon human energy.

The young human being, always eagerly learning and trying out new experiences, desperately seeking adventure and to develop its comfort zone by somehow becoming 'somebody', dares to try drugs and finds they affect them in a slightly scary, but dangerously exciting and challenging way.

They soon find themselves able to accept that challenge, begin taking more drugs and so become 'cool' amongst their friends and after a short while they laugh together about the fact that they **cannot do without their drugs!**

What is really going on is that the devious one, evil, is ensnaring their energy at the earliest possible moment in their existence.

For young humans to be introduced to drugs at such a tender age clearly demonstrates evil's malicious intent against innocent human energy as it preys upon them in their formative years, seeking out those with the sensitive genes, DNA and metabolism whose energy it can most easily damage.

So it is experimentation, bravado and possible fear of being ostracised by friends for not taking drugs that makes the young human try them, along with alcohol and tobacco.

Unwittingly those friends who are the introducers of drugs to the clean energy of the innocent one are carrying out evil's work and have become evil's henchmen.

Once drugs are introduced to the innocent's bloodstream the door to the long, lonely, downward spiral has been opened.

Soon the next stage of their drugs journey will guarantee their descent into the darkness.

Dependency

Just as the body initially rejects alcohol, especially on consuming a great deal of it, because to the body the sheer quantity becomes a 'poison', so the body initially rejects drugs.

However if the young human perseveres in taking a drug, any drug, the body will quickly become accustomed to receiving it and will become addicted to it, **evil's precise intention.**

This life shattering attack upon the energy of the young human is massive and total.

Fighting their body's initial rejection of the drug then accepting the feeling it gives them and soon finding they cannot live without it ensures the energy they are has been diverted from their true path.

Their energy becomes wayward and lost and soon belongs to evil and will remain so unless they can somehow kick their addiction to the drug.

But if their life remains difficult, if they cannot see any hope of finding or living a better life and that clear reason for them to go through the tough time of taking their energy back from drugs is missing, they will remain forever in the downward spiral that leads to the dark void.

Any system of living that allows this assault upon the energy given to humanity to continue is a system that assists evil in its war against human energy.

When you make the mistake that evil wants you to, that of reaching out with the energy you have been given to the drug and you put it inside your body, the sacred vessel you have been given to sail through this incredible journey of life within, understand that you are falling into evil's trap and taking a step down a dark, lonely road that ensures you will no longer own or manage the great gift of energy you have received.

It will be owned and managed by evil.

If you mess with evil, evil will mess with you

And sooner or later it will take away all of the energy you have been given and you will be gone – forever.

Why do you 'need' to take a drug?
To feel 'better'?
To get a 'buzz'?
To feel more 'powerful'?
To have an 'adventure'?
To get away from your life?
To be 'cool' and accepted?
Because you can't live without it?

Is your life so completely dreadful, boring, disastrous, nasty, terrifying and totally bad that you actually need to reach out to the lying, cheating trickery and false security of a drug to somehow be able to cope with it or run away from it?

If so then why on earth haven't you changed the life you have for a better one?

Because you can't see how to?

Even though you've been created as a highly intelligent being?

This is simply the indoctrination you have received from the system we live under kicking in to convince you that you are powerless to change your life, which is absolute nonsense.

You can think for yourself, can't you?

Well then, when exactly was it that you made the decision to have a lousy life that would be owned and controlled by drugs?

Your life is never totally 'locked' into any situation such as where you live, who you live with, how you live every day, what you work at, what you play at, etc., so never believe this to be so because it is you who decides whether bad things continue in your life or whether to change your life for the better through giving good, strong management to the energy you are.

If you are saying to yourself:

'I can't move from where I live because I don't have enough money', then the system is dictating to you how your life will be and this is wrong, the system has no right to dictate your life to you.

It is your energy
It was given to you and no one else
It is yours to manage while you are here
It does not belong to the system we live under
It belongs to you

With a bit of work you will find that a lack of money need never stop you doing anything with your life.

There is a wealth of information on the internet and at your local library that could easily point you in the right direction. If you still have difficulty then start asking people **outside** your current circle of 'friends' about new jobs, different places to live, other countries, how you might be able to volunteer to help people and so on.

If your life is not good, but you feel safer with it the way it is then keep in mind that you only have a tiny fragment of time here in which to do your best to get it right – and the way to get it right will come to you in your answers to **the question**:

In the moment my journey of life on earth is over what do I want to be able to say my life has been about?

Do you really want to be able to say that all you did with the greatest gift in the universe was to take more drugs than anyone else?

Think hard about what you would really like to be doing with your life.

Most of all think about the kinds of people you would like to be helping and what great and positive and beneficial effect you would like the energy you have been given to have on the people you help – because this is your way out of the drugs wilderness.

Once you have formulated this in your mind try and work out how you could possibly reach that better life and then never, ever give up trying to get there and remember that if things don't turn out quite as you hoped you can always change the way you go about trying to get there.

By doing this you will be fighting and beating evil, managing your energy well and following your true path.

Imagine yourself living that life you would much prefer to your current one.

Be careful not to fall into the trap of wanting riches, fast cars, etc., that's the system trying to ensnare your energy again by getting you to worship the money-god.

Maybe you should think of a life where you do not take drugs, where you have a really good purpose and where people respect you as a friend, so that you have people around you who you can rely on?

Whatever kind of life you think you would like to have try and imagine yourself already living it, imagine everything about it and try to feel what it would be like as best you can.

Then go back to your life as it is now and start thinking about what exactly it is you are going to have to do to get yourself to that better life.

Soon you're going to come up with some answers and then all it takes is for you to be bold and start changing your life. You have nothing to fear and always bear in mind that staying where you are and doing the same old same old will never get you to that better life, will never get you to those answers you have given in response to **the question.**

You need to be conscious that whatever is blocking you from achieving this change, possibly to a life where your energy could be of great beneficial use in helping others, is working for the very thing that wants to stop you.

Do not let it.

Don't just cave in and start saying 'I can't do this because…' or 'I can't do that because…' for this is the system's attempt to keep you locked into the life you currently have.

The Energy Thief Drugs

Drugs, like alcohol, have no energy, no life force and no power.

Put a few things to represent drugs in front of you and look at them.

If you fold your arms and look at them for the next billion years they will not have harmed you nor locked down your energy into dependency nor forced you to work all hours nor made you steal from other human beings to get the money to afford the drugs you need.

They have no energy, no life force and no power.

You were created as all three.

Drugs need you to make the mistake of reaching out to them with the energy you have been given, energising them with your energy and putting them inside your body.

Once there they immediately begin their deadly work of 'hooking' the energy you are so they can steal it away from you.

When you take drugs do you have energy? Yes?

How about when their effect has worn off? No?

So then you want to take them again?

That's because the drugs you took managed to convince you they were giving you energy when in fact they were stealing it from you and now your body is crying out for more energy because it has been stripped of its energy by the drugs.

So you take more drugs and you have that feeling of energy again, but what is really going on is that the drugs are ripping the energy out of you once more and afterwards you have no energy and your body's crying out because it's desperate to get its energy back.

So you take more drugs and they rip even more energy out of you.

You are now in the downward spiral, travelling the dark road with drugs owning and managing the energy that was given to you, you've lost the ability to manage your own energy, you've handed it over to the drugs and they are going to take you down and out of this world if they possibly can.

We could say that drugs are evil's disciples, they are energy thieves come to steal every ounce of energy that you are away from you. If you use drugs you will find they soon own your energy and it will be they who will be dictating to you how you will be whilst you are here upon the earth. And that may not be for long.

Remember that the con operated by the energy thief drugs is to get you to think **you** are in control of **it**, when all the time **it** is in control of **you.**

Drugs will ensure you lose your money, your family, your real friends and your time.

You will lose lots of time, your entire lifetime.

You will exist between one drug taking session and the next, you will live in the most dreadful of worlds, evil's living hell of drug dependency and evil will steal every last precious drop of your energy until it has taken it all from you.

You will exist as little or nothing, a shadow of the energy you were created as and sooner or later you will cease to exist at all, evil's precise intention.

Look at the 'drugs' in front of you.

They can do **nothing** and if you don't reach out to them they can never, ever damage the energy you are.

But if you make the mistake of giving them just a little of your energy, they will steal all of it and leave you with none.

They are cunning and devious energy thieves.

The Slave Trade

Those who grow drugs seed the slave trade.

Those who make drugs create the slave trade.

Those who deliver drugs spread the slave trade.

Those who buy and sell drugs are the slave traders.

Those who cannot live without drugs are the slaves.

When you see the drug dealers, those you misguidedly think are your friends, recognise evil's agents for who they really are, the slave traders.

It doesn't matter that they don't think of themselves as slave traders, but it's the simple reality of what they are - the agents of evil as it plies its trade over its slaves.

They are working on evil's behalf and giving it the opportunity to get into control of and extinguish your energy even as they laugh and tell you,

'This'll give you a great buzz'
'This is the latest, it's the best'
'This is the way to go'
'Go on, try some'
'Have the first one free.......'

All they have to do is plant the idea in your mind that drugs are the right thing for you to give your energy to and it's so very, very easy for them to do so by telling you 'this will make you feel better'.

'Better'?

You'll certainly feel different, but you will never feel 'better'!

Why do you think drugs are banned?

Why do you think they have been made illegal?

Because they're good for you?

No!

They are not banned in order to stop you having a good time, there are hundreds of ways you can have a good time that don't involve drugs.

Drugs are banned because they will turn your life into a living nightmare.

And they will steal the energy you have been given and lock it into a lifetime of slavery.

If you simply hand over your great gift of energy to drugs you guarantee you will never be anything more than a slave trader's slave travelling a long, dark, lonely road for your entire lifetime.

A better life awaits you, but to get there you will have to manage your energy in a completely different way than you have been and start helping other people.

This is your route back from the wilderness of drug dependency to that better life.

You have to be bold, you have to be strong, but in the moment you turn and help someone you are on your way and all the time you continue to help other human beings you will be beating evil.

You are the Energy!

Don't Let The Energy Thieves Win!

Tobacco

Always think of yourself as the centre of your energy and that out there in our world are countless cunning, devious and dangerous energy thieves determined to steal your energy so they can destroy your life. Most energy thieves have no energy, no life force and no power until you give them some of yours and then they'll steal it all!

Tobacco is the Third Henchman in Evil's Deadly Trilogy.

The Third Horseman of your Apocalypse.

If you're using alcohol, drugs and tobacco then as actor David Strathairn said in the movie of the same name:

'Good night and good luck.'

Tobacco is the thief the system wants to attract our attention towards to divert it away from alcohol and drugs and the misery they are wreaking upon human energy. That's why there has been the big smokescreen of a 'battle' going on against the giant tobacco companies and why there are big health warnings on packs of cigarettes.

And this battle and the massive court cases that have been won have made little difference to the total amount of tobacco being smoked in our world because the fight against the tobacco companies is a game of smoke and mirrors.

If tobacco sales are falling in one country the tobacco companies use heavy marketing to increase sales in another.

Also you don't see great big warning signs on bottles of alcohol, do you?

Why not?

Because the system's got us looking at tobacco.

Tobacco is 'the insidious one' and behind it stands the devious one, evil.

Tobacco is insidious not only because it has the capability of killing you, but the smoke from your cigarette, 'second hand smoke', along with the smoke you exhale, can be extremely harmful to those around you.

And now the deadliness of tertiary exposure, 'third hand smoke' has been proved with the poisons and toxins from cigarette smoke lingering on nearby surfaces, fabrics or hair and yet most people do not know about this and its deadly risk to small children.

Pregnant women are particularly at risk if they are in contact with people who have been smoking and are consequently carrying toxic matter in their hair or clothing.

Tobacco truly is an insidious energy thief with its triple ability to damage you and others.

The air we breathe, pure and clean, was given as a birthright to all human beings as one of our critical life support systems.

The cleaner the air we breathe the better, the more polluted it is the worse for our health.

If you smoke tobacco you pollute everyone's air – and you don't need to be smoking anywhere near them to do this, your smoke pollutes the atmosphere and consequently you are damaging the air that was given to all of humanity.

If the billions of human beings who smoke tobacco stopped smoking might that also reduce global warming as well as cleaning up the air we all breathe?

The Energy Thief Tobacco

When you smoked your very first cigarette, did you like it?

Or did you find it distasteful, those first few puffs?

The first time you inhaled tobacco smoke did you cough and choke or feel nauseous?

Didn't you recognise the warning signs from your body telling you that it didn't want you to put that smoke, which it regarded as poison, inside yourself?

In those first few cigarettes did you ever throw up?

Wasn't that a big enough warning sign to you from your body?

The problem was that in a very short time your body went from hating tobacco smoke to liking it as it became addicted to it.

Tobacco smoke began to numb your body and your mind and you became convinced you needed it because you thought it made you feel 'better', which it never did.

The truth is that it was tobacco that needed you to reach out to it with your energy before it was able to begin its deadly work upon you.

The great con of the energy thief was on.

Once in a very blue moon I go for a full medical check up and I'm fairly sure they're not going to find anything, unless there's something going on I have no knowledge of, which hopefully there won't be.

I get asked a lot of questions about my health and my medical history and I always do pretty well with these.

And then comes the tobacco question:

'Do you smoke?'

'No, I don't smoke.'

(Ha-ha, got you! I don't smoke and I'm as healthy as can be!).

And then comes the follow up question:

'Did you ever smoke?'

'Well…yes, I did…once…but it was a long time ago.'

In that moment the person asking the questions changes, they metamorphose into some kind of superior, power being and fix me with a steadfast eagle stare.

'When did you smoke?'

'Well, I smoked a bit in my teens.'

Still the icy stare remains.

'When, precisely did you smoke?'

'From around 16 to 18 I suppose.'

'You need to be precise and I need to know what you smoked.'

'Well I first smoked a cigarette I guess when I was 10, you know, behind the bicycle sheds at school, but I didn't smoke again until my mid-teens.'

'So what did you smoke?'

'Cigarettes and then a pipe for a while when I was 18, it was fashionable then.'

All of this is being written down and now my medical examiner knows they will have to look for the spot on my lung that evil put there all that time ago that could suddenly explode out of nowhere as lung cancer and kill me.

You see it's always true of energy thieves that if they can't nail your energy on their first attempt they more than likely will sometime later on in your life and when they do it will definitely be before your time to leave.

And that spot of cancer was put on your lung by you after you were tricked by evil into taking the smoke from the energy thief tobacco into your lungs.

You put that spot there when you and your friends smoked all that time ago, when smoking seemed so cool, when you were out of step if you didn't smoke, when you saw your idols smoking in the movies, on television, in magazines and thought it would be cool to be like them.

And back then you were so full of energy you felt you could live forever.

You never thought that 30 would come, or 40, or 50 and that if you did live that long it would never be **you** who would get cancer.

But maybe you've got it now only you just don't know it and maybe you won't know it until it's too late.

Why on earth would you want to pay the supreme price of having your existence ended just because you were conned into entering your life ticket into the alcohol, drugs and tobacco lottery?

The only lottery prizes these three massive energy thieves ever pay out are your enslavement into dependency and the total theft and destruction of your energy so that it is they who dictate how you will be while you are here and not you.

You did not receive the great gift of life for you to test and keep on testing your body to see how much alcohol, drugs and tobacco it can withstand.

If you are determined to test it to see how much it can withstand you will increasingly damage the vessel you live in and if you keep on testing it you will damage that vessel beyond repair.

'Smoking damages nearly every organ in the human body, is linked to at least 15 different cancers and accounts for some 30% of all cancer deaths.'   American Cancer Society

In 2006 the **US Surgeon General** determined:

'There is no risk-free level of exposure to second hand smoke and that breathing even a little second hand smoke poses a risk to your health because it is toxic and poisonous.'

The World Health Organisation (WHO) states:

'Cigarettes kill half of all lifetime users.
Half die in middle age, between 35 and 69 years old.
Tobacco kills more than AIDS, legal drugs, illegal drugs, road accidents, murder and suicide combined.'

'Of everyone alive today 500,000,000 (half a billion) will eventually be killed by tobacco.'

Report for the **Tobacco Advisory Council,** 1978:

"...with a general lengthening of the expectation of life we really need something for people to die of..."

Source: World Health Organisation (WHO)

If you rid your life of the energy thief tobacco the benefits to your health kick in very quickly.

Your risk of cancer, lung and heart disease falls and stress on your heart is reduced.

The risk of circulatory problems resulting in gangrene or amputation is reduced.

The health of your skin and whiteness of your teeth will improve.

Women improve their chances of a healthy pregnancy and healthy baby.

Your smoker's cough will subside.

You will be able to taste things you were not able to taste before.

You will no longer smell of smoke.

All those doubts you may have had about yourself will begin to disappear as you gain increasing confidence in your self-image.

You will no longer be harming those around you.

You will save a heck of a lot of money.

Always keep these things in the forefront of your mind at all times and always remember:

It's up to you – it's your energy

You are the Energy!

Don't Let The Energy Thieves Win!

Bullying

Always think of yourself as the centre of your energy and that out there in our world are countless cunning, devious and dangerous energy thieves determined to steal your energy so they can destroy your life. Most energy thieves have no energy, no life force and no power until you give them some of yours and then they'll steal it all!

**Bullies think they are strong
because they can dominate the weak**

**Bullies are extremely weak
They travel a dark road**

Whether they need to be in a gang to carry out their bullying or they bully individual people on their own, every time they make another human being's life miserable bullies prove how weak they are.

Bullies are giving in to the temptation from the dark side because bullying human beings is nothing less than the work of evil.

It is evil the bullies work for and you can see this for yourself once you understand what is happening to their energy.

Don't let the training you receive from the system encourage you to believe that it is right we human beings should live by the 'law of the jungle' and it is the physically strong who are guaranteed to succeed through bullying, dominating or controlling the weak.

This is a deadly con, a trap for your energy set by evil to get you to set out down a dark road to a less than enjoyable life.

Only the weak pick on the weak, the strong defend everyone

Because deep down inside those who bully others are scared or unhappy in their lives they think that when they make others scared or unhappy they are somehow making their own lives better, which is nothing but dangerous nonsense borne of system trickery.

The bully feels they are gaining 'power' from and over others, this is the con run by the energy thief bullying for they are not gaining 'power' at all by taking it from others - they are losing it!

The first time they bully someone they sense a feeling they have not felt before which cons them into thinking it's a good feeling, but it cannot be because it comes from dominating another human being and making them miserable, which no one has the right to do and is completely the wrong way for the bully to be managing their energy.

However it may be the only 'comfort' type of feeling they've ever known, something they can do on their own that makes them feel 'secure' and 'in charge' of their energy, perhaps for the very first time. This is the beginning of building the wrong kind of comfort zone, one that involves hurting other human beings.

Maybe their parents set them the example of bullying and they know nothing else.

Their bullying can also be triggered through a yearning to establish themselves as 'somebody' and instead of achieving this through doing spectacularly good and great deeds to help their fellow human beings they make the mistake of hurting others which means all they have succeeded in becoming is 'nobody'.

The more they bully the more that 'comforting' feeling turns into one of false satisfaction and so they fall for the con and want that feeling more and more.

It's like a drug, but when they bully someone and they damage that person's energy – they also damage their own energy – they do not gain energy from the person they bully, they only think they do for that is the con being operated against them.

What is happening is that both of them are losing their energy.

The bully loses the great gift of energy they have received to bullying and the person being bullied loses energy through being bullied.

Both of them lose.

But the bully loses the most by far because they have mis-managed their energy and consequently let their existence fall into a dark downward spiral that will ensure theirs is a miserable and unhappy existence of benefit to no one, least of all themselves.

The one who is being bullied will recover whenever they are away from the bully. The bully will never, ever recover for as long as they continue bullying.

The energy thief bullying is leading them down a dark road on which there will only be more and more energy loss through more and more bullying until all of the energy that was given to the bully has been surrendered to evil.

As the bully's life unfolds and they follow this road down into the dark void they will find their life disintegrates around them.

They will be unable to enjoy good, loving, rewarding and lasting relationships with anyone.

They will be unable to hold down a job.

The only 'friends' they will have are other bullies who will turn on them in a second if they show weakness and sooner or later, most probably sooner, because their life is false and without proper meaning and purpose they will begin directing their energy towards the things they think are going to 'help' them feel 'better' such as alcohol, drugs, tobacco, gambling and crime.

Bullying is evil, it is designed to trap the energy of the bully and ensure they can never find their true path in this world.

It is a massive diversion of their great gift of energy.

If you promote evil your energy is under the control of evil and is no longer managed by you, it only feels as if it is because you are falling for the con.

If you mess with evil, evil will mess with you.

This means that if you continue to bully others evil will own the energy that you are and ensure you face a lonely, dark and hopeless life, which is all it wants you to have.

Evil will have succeeded in knocking you off course and will have stopped you from ever finding your true path and purpose in this world.

The bully misguidedly thinks their life is good and that they are happy.

It's not their fault because they don't understand what they're messing with and what has taken over the management of their energy.

Evil's con lies in getting them to believe they are doing the right thing, living the right way and getting stronger when the fact is their life is sinking into the darkness and they are getting weaker and becoming more and more unhappy deep down inside.

Instead of using their strength and energy to do good, they are using it to do evil, which only creates more pain for themselves.

Instead of using their strength to protect the weak and gain respect in their community so that doors begin to open to them and their life goes forward positively, they attack those who are defenceless, destroying their own energy in the process and ensuring the only respect they earn is the false 'respect' of fear and so the doors of their community remain very firmly closed to them.

How much better it would be for the bully to channel their energy into a far tougher challenge, that of helping and protecting others, especially those they bully. If they cannot do this they prove to everyone including themselves how weak they really are.

If they helped others, helped everyone they could and got themselves off the dark road and reversed the downward spiral and began to nurture and grow their energy in a vastly better way they could make their lives far more fulfilling and be happy in the knowledge they had earned real respect within their community.

This way, on the road of good, lies a life of great possibilities.
The bullying way, on the dark road, lies a life in the darkness.

As soon as the bully changes the road they're on and starts helping those they have been bullying they immediately take their energy back from evil and take a giant step off the dark road back towards the road of good, the road of light, the road of happiness and contentment.

But evil will keep trying to con them back onto the dark road.

It never, ever gives up.

That is a mark of how hard it can be to stay on the road of good, the road for those who are not just physically tough.

Maybe they will feel silly helping those they have been bullying.

Maybe they will prefer that strange false feeling of security and comfort generated through their bullying to the feeling they get on the road of good, which is all part of the con to get them to turn back to bullying.

Maybe their co-bullies will turn on them like a pack of animals and make it truly difficult for them to get off the dark road, as happens in gang culture, if they attempt to stop bullying and start defending and helping the defenceless.

Following the road of good is only for truly tough people
It's far tougher than following the road of evil

The road of good is only for you if you are really tough deep down inside because it's a road full of challenges and tricks and traps and countless energy thieves constantly thrown at you to try to trip you up.

The road of good is tough to follow, the road of evil is easy

The problem with setting your life off down the dark road through bullying is that there are only two roads you can follow in this world, the road of good or the road of evil.

If you follow the dark road it will lead you more and more to lying, cheating, stealing, swindling, alcohol abuse, drug taking, gambling, criminality, punishment, pain and unhappiness.

During all of this throughout your life you will think you are in control of the energy you have been given, but the reality is that you will be completely out of control of it, this is the con.

You are only ever in charge of the energy you have been given when you deliberately manage it well and follow the hard road, the road of good.

As you follow the dark road, being drawn ever closer to evil, you will be conned into feeling that this is the right thing for you to be doing. But you will become less and less capable of changing your life for the better because you will be losing more and more energy all the time to evil, until finally evil owns all of your energy and your entire being and there is no way back for you.

I have met truly evil human beings, people you would not want to be in the same room with because the energy coming off them was so evil, thick, heavy and impenetrable.

They had served the darkness all of their lives.

Why would you want to?

The real power given to you is not your physical power, it's the power to direct the energy you have been given towards doing good, to act from the vast life powers of love and compassion within you for your fellow human beings and to help and protect them in every way that you can.

In this way they will soon become your friends and the more real friends you have the larger your comfort zone becomes.

Who knows, one day they may even repay your kindness by helping you, but don't help them just because you're looking for some kind of reward. Help them because you genuinely want to and then walk away and see what happens over time.

If you help others, in whatever way you can, the reward comes both inside you and through the doors that will open to you in your community, your society.

Doors that will not open to the bully.

You will then be nurturing and growing the energy that you are.

This will make you far happier and far more contented with your life.

You will also be helping to nurture and grow the energy of those around you. This in turn will make them happier and more contented with their lives. This is the great power you have been given.

I am helping you right now to grasp the opportunity to nurture and grow your energy, which in turn makes my energy grow stronger, so I am happier and more contented and we both benefit.

It is all so very simple, but so very powerful, precisely the opposite of what the system we live under tries to get us to believe in as being 'power'.

And by using your energy, your power, in this way you will begin to gain the respect of everyone around you.

This respect is completely different from the 'respect' the bully feels they are generating because that is a false respect borne of fear.

This is the kind of respect that means people will want to know you, they don't want to know a bully.

This kind of respect means people will become your friends.

This kind of respect means people will help you.

They will not help a bully, at least not of their own free will.

This kind of respect means people will offer you good things, maybe better education, maybe a survival course that they otherwise wouldn't want you on because your bullying makes you a risk, maybe a sailing holiday on an ocean going yacht, maybe a job, maybe a career, maybe some happiness.

The possibilities are never ending.

For the bully these things quickly become less and less possible because the so called 'respect' they think they are gaining through their bullying in reality means they are generating nothing but disrespect.

I was at school with a lot of bullies and I was bullied day and night from a young age until around the age of 16 when my body did an 'Incredible Hulk' act and I knocked the living daylights out of someone who tried to bully me.

Then the bullying stopped, because bullies **only bully those they can bully easily, those who they think can't fight back.**

They will never try to bully those they know can fight back in a big way.

Bullies are weak – they just don't know they are

But the bullies who stopped bullying me then turned on those who were younger and weaker than I was and began bullying them and making their lives miserable instead.

So I said to a number of friends that if we got together we could stop all the bullies and life would become better for everyone.

And that's exactly what we did.

Whenever anyone bullied someone, I or one of my friends would go and give them a good thumping and tell them that this was what they would get until they stopped their bullying.

And guess what?

All the bullying stopped, we stamped it out of our school.

The bullies then applied their energy to doing good things, like academic learning or sport or helping others in whatever way they could.

They took their energy back from evil and stepped off the dark road onto the road of good and consequently grew into better human beings and their lives went forward positively.

In this way they avoided the slide into a lifetime of pain in the darkness.

Bullying is far more negative for those who do the bullying than it is for those who are bullied

I am not recommending that you go around thumping bullies, because these days that will be an offence, it wasn't when I was at school.

You need to find another, better way to stamp out bullying.

Taking the bully out of their environment and getting them to survive on their own is a really good way, maybe get them on a survival course, a really tough one!

It is possible to stop bullying, whether it's physical or mental bullying, but it takes strong human beings to manage the energy they are in a different and better way to either bully the bullies, so they experience what they are meting out to others, or to explain to them how they are travelling down the dark road and working for evil which will only lead them to a life of more and more pain.

And is that what they really want?

I have seen this work well if you can get the bullies to listen.

Change Yourself

If you are the object of bullying, you must try to change yourself or your situation because something about you is attracting the bullies.

Change your appearance, your clothes, what you eat, what you talk about, where you go, what you do, completely change how you appear to others so you don't attract the bullies.

Was it your fear that was attracting them?

Were you too quiet and unassuming and therefore an 'easy target'?

Make as many changes as you can, throw yourself into different things, change your daily routines and be bold when you do this.

You need to take charge of your energy by making sure it is you who changes your situation – do not let it continue as it is.

You need to work out what all the things about you are that have been attracting the bullies to you and change them.

And if you are someone who sees bullying going on, whatever kind of bullying it is, you need to stop it. The very act of doing so means you are managing your energy well by helping those who are being bullied.

In many instances this can be easier said than done, but you need to do **something** to stop it.

You can find organisations that help with bullying on the internet and bullying can be reported to the police as physical assault.

We are all duty bound to stamp out bullying wherever and whenever we come across it. When we turn our backs and do nothing what we are really doing is allowing evil to flourish and damage the energy of everyone around us.

You are the Energy!

Don't Let The Energy Thieves Win!

Stealing

Always think of yourself as the centre of your energy and that out there in our world are countless cunning, devious and dangerous energy thieves determined to steal your energy so they can destroy your life. Most energy thieves have no energy, no life force and no power until you give them some of yours and then they'll steal it all!

Stealing is similar to bullying in many respects and there can be a number of drivers behind stealing including greed, jealousy, monetary gain, a feeling of inadequacy, a need for a challenge or a perverted desire to damage another human being.

Stealing is the living of a lie that ensures the energy of the person who steals has moved a long way from their true path and in consequence their lives are riddled with problems, not least a deep kind of self-mistrust in their ability to live any kind of 'normal' life as they travel their dark road.

They will tell lie after lie when confronted with their thievery, compounding their energy loss and ensuring they lose the inner strength they were given that would have helped them find their true path now that the energy thief stealing is controlling everything they do in life.

Stealing can become its own drug and is all too often used to gain money to buy drugs, so now there are two energy thieves operating, the one is stealing the thief's energy through their drug dependency and the other is stealing their energy by making them unable to stop stealing.

The one habit feeds the other so their life becomes imprisoned as they travel around and around this vicious circle and cannot break out of it.

What is it the thief wants to be able to say in answer to **the question** on page 8?

That what they did with the greatest gift in the universe, a gift that should have been treasured and nurtured, was to spend their tiny

80

fragment of time here on earth stealing and making other human being's lives miserable?

That's it?

That is the sum total of what they learned and achieved during their time here on earth?

What an incredible waste of the most precious of gifts!

What staggering success for the energy thief stealing!

Stealing from another human being brings trauma to that person and is often the intention of the thief. Hatred or envy (more energy thieves) for those who possess what the thief does not can often be the driver of their crime.

The victims come home to find their house has been broken into and prize possessions that meant a lot to them are gone.

It's like a black hole, a void suddenly appearing in their lives and the thought that a stranger has been in their house and what might have happened had they either been at home or arrived home earlier can affect them badly.

We can easily see the dark downwards spiral of the devious chain of evil stealing the energy of a thief who needs money to fund a drug habit as well as from those the thief steals from:

Drug Habit = Stealing = Victim in Trauma = Thief in Darkness

Yet there are many thieves who do not take drugs, but who are hooked on stealing through greed or who find their crime an exciting challenge.

One thief perpetrated years of multiple thefts in the North East of England. He had studied all the forensic programmes on television and had worked hard to ensure he never left any forensic evidence at the scene of his crimes and was only eventually caught through having made a simple mistake.

He once even made himself a bacon sandwich in a house he robbed.

But he did not perpetrate these crimes for money because the police retrieved lots of stolen goods at both his and his mother's houses, he was simply hooked on the challenge.

He could have worked for the security services or the police outsmarting other criminals or he could have joined special forces in the military or become a mountaineer or a sportsman of some description if his life lacked a challenge.

But no, he had to fall into the trap of the energy thief and have his energy diverted from its true path by getting hooked on stealing and making the lives of those he robbed miserable.

And now he's in prison.

Doubtless he thinks that it was he who got himself there, but in reality it was evil operating through the energy thief stealing that tricked him into thinking he was managing his energy really well, when in reality the energy thief had taken over managing his energy whilst running its successful con on him.

The problem is that stealing is like a drug.

Once you start stealing you can't stop, it's the same as lying which seems the 'easy way out' of taking responsibility for doing good with your energy.

Once you find you can steal and sell the stolen goods to get the money to buy what you need instead of working for it the die has been cast for you and your life here on earth.

And once your thought process starts working out how to steal then a far bigger thief than you will ever be has swung into operation as thinking about stealing begins to drug your senses.

Stealing becomes your reality as the con kids you that you are still in charge of the energy you are and it certainly seems so because you feel you're actually doing something constructive, you're gaining, you're winning.

The truth is you are doing something destructive both to your energy and the energy of others, you are not gaining, you are losing your energy, your life, your time here.

You are only really in charge of your energy when you are managing it well.

When you manage your energy badly something else is in charge of it.

But it was you who gave your energy away by managing it badly and so it is you who can take it back to yourself.

Only when you direct the energy you have been given down the road of good are you managing the energy that you are in the best possible way and giving yourself the chance of finding your true purpose, fulfilment, contentment and happiness.

Instead of making other people's lives miserable just because your own is why not work with a security firm advising people how to make their homes more secure?

Then you are helping people with your knowledge by stopping others stealing from them.

This is only one possibility, but were you to take any kind of a step like this permanently in your life you would have changed the road you're on and be setting out towards your true purpose by taking your energy back to yourself from the energy thief stealing.

If you are ingenious enough to work out ways to steal you are ingenious enough to work out ways to make a better life for yourself.

You are the Energy!

Don't Let The Energy Thieves Win!

Gambling

Always think of yourself as the centre of your energy and that out there in our world are countless cunning, devious and dangerous energy thieves determined to steal your energy so they can destroy your life. Most energy thieves have no energy, no life force and no power until you give them some of yours and then they'll steal it all!

The main lure of the energy thief gambling is to win big, but it is a far more devious thief than that and will attack you in multiple ways so that it can take control of your energy.

You gamble to win and maybe you do win now and again, but each time you gamble with your winnings you find you gradually lose them.

The thief keeps kidding you into believing you can get your money back by gambling more and more, but you never will because the gambling industry ensures the odds are always stacked against you and despite your occasional wins:

If you keep on gambling you guarantee that you will lose!

When you go to a casino or bet on a horse race understand that the people you gamble with are in business to make money out of you. If people like you were to win all the time those organisations you bet with would quickly be out of business.

They will always make money out of you, it is their business to do so.

The truth is that only a very small percentage of people win, as in any lottery, because the odds are stacked against you to make sure that 'the house always wins'.

Occasionally you or someone you hear of will have a big win and this will encourage you, but try taking a look at the sheer amount of people who don't win. It vastly exceeds the amount of those who do.

The thief will keep calling you to gamble more and more by luring you with these thoughts:

<u>Lure</u> 1:

Wouldn't it be great to have a big win?
Think of all the things you could do with the money!

<u>Lure</u> 2:

You heard about someone who won big.
So why shouldn't you?

<u>Lure</u> 3:

If you win big you can pay off all your debts!

But the truth is that your gambling habit will only increase your debts!

As soon as the energy thief gambling begins to control your energy you will become desperate to gamble more and more.

With these three lures enticing and driving you in the anticipation and excitement of the act of gambling and the possibility of having that big win evil will quickly hook your energy to its henchman gambling.

When you feel unhappy, bored, angry or depressed you turn to gambling for excitement and find you somehow feel safer when you're gambling than when you're not gambling.

The con the energy thief is running on you is working well.

And if you do have a win it will only accelerate your desire to gamble more because you've proved you can win and if you were to have just one more really big win your problems would be solved and your life would be complete.

It will never happen, the thief will see to it by making sure you keep gambling and that you keep losing because of the way those odds are stacked against you.

You will go home with little or no money, usually with none, those businesses you pay your money over to when you gamble will ensure it is taken from you.

And having lost your money you may seek revenge against gambling in your desperation to get it back and revenge, another energy thief, takes over the energy you are so you begin to borrow money to gamble so you can 'get even' and you lose that too.

You use up all of your cash and credit and mortgage your home and use that money in a desperate attempt to achieve the big win you crave and the more small wins you have the further the thief is encouraging you down the dark road and the more money you lose the more angry and desperate for 'revenge' you become.

Your gambling affects everyone in your family, you never have any money to give them, instead you always want money from them.

You consistently lie to your family and friends that 'everything's alright' and you're 'doing well'.

The thief has you lying so that you are living a lie and your life is turning into an empty shell in consequence.

You begin drinking alcohol to excess to shore up your flagging confidence, to make you feel 'better'.

You start taking drugs for the same reason, but alcohol and drugs do not make you feel 'better', they only ever make you feel different and you cannot stand their effects wearing off as you find yourself having to face reality each time they do, so you spend more and more money on alcohol and drugs so they can keep you in that state of feeling 'better'.

Now the thief is gaining total control and power over your energy because it has you losing your money and energy to alcohol, drugs, gambling, anger, revenge and desperation as it sends the energy you are further and further down into the dark void.

Once it has you convinced that you can gamble your way out of your dire financial situation it has won, the con is complete, evil has wreaked its devious work upon you, spinning the energy that was given to you around and around in the most painful of dark downwards spirals.

Your gambling problem consumes your life and turns it into hell on earth.

You have massive debts.
You become homeless.
You lose those who were closest to you.
You are an alcoholic.
You are a drug addict.
Your health is a disaster.
You do not realise you are on your way out of this world.

The plan of evil, to divert the energy that was given to you as far from your true path as possible so you cannot find and live out your true purpose, is to ultimately get your energy off this planet so that evil becomes the victor in the battle over the great gift of energy you have received.

And you will never know true happiness, contentment and fulfilment, your life will be beneficial to no one, least of all you and you will exist in an unforgiving world that drives you down the dark road to the end of your existence, which will most probably be long before your time.

Your only chance, your only way out is through a proper understanding of what is really happening to you, that you are under the attack of evil and its cohorts of darkness, that they are winning and that you do not have much time left in which to stop them.

Understand that the urge to gamble does not come from the real you, it comes from the energy thief gambling and the lures it throws out to you, the false promises of great riches, the lies it tells you.

Why would you ever believe a liar?

Understand that you cannot win consistently because of the way the odds are deliberately stacked against you by the businesses whose job it is to make money out of you.

They are not here to give you money, only to ensure you consistently lose it.

Understand that gambling is not the game it appears to be, it's a really tough business and it will always devour every penny of the money you throw at it.

Understand the reality of money being only a transient thing that comes into one hand and goes out of the other, you come here with none and you leave here with none, so why would you let it dictate to you how you will be whilst you are here?

Understand that you are also a transient being undertaking a part of your journey of learning here on earth and that you are here for what is in reality a very short space of time and you only have this one chance to use the great gift of energy you have received in the best possible way.

And gambling is definitely not the best possible way.

You need to reach deep inside yourself and access and deploy the great weapon of being able to give instant good, strong management and guidance to the energy that you are.

Immediately you think about gambling move your energy away from that thought, banish it from your being and go and help someone in whatever way you can, which you have not been doing, have you?

You have just been supposedly 'helping' yourself through gambling.

When gambling, alcohol and drugs call out to you immediately recognise that the cohorts of darkness are coming straight at your heart to kill you if they can and instantly direct the energy that you are away from them – go and help someone.

Then keep helping people as much as you can all of the time, force yourself to manage the energy that you are down the road of good so that you leave these deadly energy thieves behind in the past where all of them, including gambling, will remain powerless to hurt you.

For you the road of good will not be easy because the thief will keep calling out to you, but the road will only be hard until you have travelled a little way down it, for soon you will have rid yourself of the shackles of the energy thieves who were stealing your life from you and you will find you now only want to walk that new road you have put yourself on.

And you will find some or possibly all of these things beginning to happen to you:

Your debts start to fall and in time they vanish all together.

Your family will give you love and respect for how you have changed your life for the better, so will your friends.

Your existence will not have ended, though you came close.

Your health will improve dramatically.

That great deep seated fear of failure within that was driving you will disappear.

It will be replaced by a feeling of calm, a growing reassurance that you are managing your energy and your life well.

Through being honest with yourself and others you will become well thought of and doors will begin to open to you.

You will have won the great battle against evil and you will be walking the path of good. You will have found your true path and be on your way to your true purpose.

You may have helped one heck of a lot of human beings beat the very same gambling problem and you will have given your life true value and meaning.

You have now gained perspective on what is really happening to you and know you have a choice between letting evil take the greatest gift in the universe away from you or putting the privilege of the great gift of energy that you have received to the best possible use while you are here and so beat the energy thief gambling.

You are the Energy!

Don't Let The Energy Thieves Win!

Gangs

Always think of yourself as the centre of your energy and that out there in our world are countless cunning, devious and dangerous energy thieves determined to steal your energy so they can destroy your life. Most energy thieves have no energy, no life force and no power until you give them some of yours and then they'll steal it all!

The way the system we live under dominates your life can mean that from a young age you are being groomed to accept gang culture as being 'normal' depending on the circumstances of where you live, what you've been taught about life and what is going on around you.

Gangs may rule the neighbourhood you live in and from a very young age you may hear talk of them and think they represent normality.

Sooner or later you're going to meet them on the street.

These seemingly tough people may immediately become your role models because they appear to have 'power', to be exciting and 'in control' of everything.

If there is nothing else going on in your life that you find satisfying then gangs may look inviting.

Perhaps life has already been tough and you've been bullied or abused or you've had to witness or endure what gangs dish out and learned to accept it until you reach the age where almost inevitably their spider's web touches you.

In that moment be aware that your great gift of energy is about to be stolen from you.

Gangs often beat up or kill people who refuse to join them.

This indicates a deadly energy thief that is desperate to consume and control the energy of others.

A gang may get you to join them by frightening you or by physical force or by blackmailing and threatening you, your life or your family. Let's look at how a gang might start.

Young people who are disenfranchised, unloved and unhappy with lives that are immersed in and dictated to by alcohol, drugs, tobacco and stealing, who have 'nothing to do' and not much hope of their lives getting any better find themselves automatically bonding and banding together.

They form groups within which they discover a kind of friendship, a camaraderie, a feeling of security, a bond they haven't experienced before and all of a sudden they have a new purpose and some hope of 'being somebody', of actually getting somewhere in life.

The 'gang' has already begun stealing their energy.

As their gang becomes stronger in number and bolder in consequence they suddenly find they come up against another gang and that the two gangs hate each other.

Why?

Because they are competing forces, this is the law of the jungle in all its glory, kept in place by the system we live under as it sets one group of human beings against another for no reason other than to get them to expend their energy on something that will do nothing but create misery for themselves and others.

In this way their energy is being 'controlled' by the system.

So you, the gang member having to hate this other gang or be set upon by your own gang if you don't, have no option but to fight the other gang. This will swiftly escalate into serious assault involving the use of knives, guns and other weapons.

When groups of young people fight each other they lose their energy to each other and become diverted from their true path

91

Once you have fought on behalf of the gang your life as a gang member is confirmed and from then on your energy will be ruled by a whole host of energy thieves including alcohol, drugs, tobacco, knives, guns, hatred, jealousy, greed, anger, bullying, joy riding, anti-social behaviour, criminal acts, pain and of course – evil.

This is the battleground, which you never recognised because no one warned you about it and yet you're standing on the battleground because you're in the gang and every day evil is sending all of these energy thieves against you to steal your energy.

Pretty soon you, the gang member, do not know which way is up as your life is turned into abusing drugs, dealing drugs, drinking alcohol to oblivion, stealing, committing criminal acts and fighting other gangs.

The energy that you were created as has now been totally consumed by the gang and pretty soon the gang is all you know or remember and you believe that you're actually 'happy', because you have 'purpose', that recognition, that feeling of security, that feeling of being wanted, of being part of something, of at last being 'somebody'.

And worst of all you believe you have 'respect' from your community, when all you really have is their fear.

And in consequence of this feeling of 'happiness' and 'respect' you give all of your misguided 'loyalty' to the very thing that is actually taking your energy and your life away from you and leading you down a darker and darker road brimming over with danger to you and to others.

This is the con run by the energy thief the gang to get you to think that you're in charge of your energy and that all you want to do is stay in the gang. The problem is that it is the gang that is in charge of your energy and so leaving the gang would be a big problem for you.

Have a good think about whether you could ever leave your gang if you wanted to.

Forget about the fact you don't want to leave your gang for a minute, just ask yourself that if you did want to leave could you actually do it?

No, of course you couldn't.

You would certainly be beaten up by the other gang members or worse.

It's like an addiction, the power of evil over your energy makes it really tough to stop and you can't just walk away because you would probably be risking your life if you tried to.

So you stay 'loyal' to the gang, but it's not real loyalty.

Loyalty to the Gang = Fear

This is the way that evil works to steal and contain your energy and use it for its own purposes so you cannot use it for your own.

Evil is running a major con on you by getting you to think you're in control of everything to do with your gang life, but the truth is **gang life is in control of you and so you have lost any other options of what you can do with your life.**

If your gang was to get rid of all of its weapons right now, no more knives, guns, bullets, baseball bats, etc., what is the first thing that is going to come at you?

Other gangs!

So again you cannot put down your weapons and leave the gang **through fear!**

First the gang takes your energy from you to bring itself into being as some sort of 'power' and then it exercises that power over you and controls everything you do.

Yet you actually think that you are in control of your energy and you are so convinced you are you simply cannot see the reality that:

The Gang is the Energy Thief!

How about this?

No gang members = No gang!

Sound stupid?

It means that, just as with any energy thief, if there's no one giving their energy to it the gang ceases to exist and it cannot steal any gang member's energy away from them and they will be free to live **as they want to.**

Every energy thief that a human being takes their energy away from can no longer steal their energy!

So does this mean a gang is some sort of a chain of evil?

Most certainly.

Most gangs operate evil practices by their very nature.

And most gang members end up in prison at some time, losing all of their energy to the prison system and getting criminal records and the limitations that places upon them in society for the rest of their lives.

All because of the gang.

If you don't give your energy to evil it finds it difficult to harm you, but once you give evil your energy it will take all of it away from you.

The gang is an energy thief that begins operating on you as soon as you join it so that it can control the energy that was given to you and steal it from you forever.

The Gang

Dig yourself a large hole, climb into it, put on a hard hat, wait for the bomb to drop and never travel further than the bottom of your garden.

Dig yourself a large hole:	Want to be a gang member
Climb into it:	Become a gang member
Put on a hard hat:	Nothing matters but the gang
Wait for the bomb to drop:	Just keep doing the same old thing for the sake of the gang
Make sure you never travel further than the bottom of your garden:	Never venture outside the 'security' of the gang

Live out your entire existence having the gang dictate what you will do and what you won't do with the energy that belongs to you.

Let the energy thief that is the gang succeed in stealing your energy so you never get to understand there is a far better, far more beneficial and fulfilling life out there for you if only you would take your energy back from the gang and start directing the energy you are down the road of good.

Gang Busters

Let's say that in your gang there are fifty members and together you are committing crimes, putting fear into people and completely wasting your great gift of life by following the dark road evil wants you to.

That is a huge amount of human energy being managed by evil.

And let's say that you, the individual gang member, go out right now and help someone in your community, all you do is help one person in whatever good way you can and walk away.

And let's call doing this '**1 help**'.

Your giving them this help in fact helps you both.

They benefit from the **1 help** given and you benefit from the satisfaction inside from having given them your help plus the fact that you have not been following the road of evil while you were doing so.

Then let's say that, following your magnificent example, all fifty of you go out and you each help someone in a really good way and walk away with the benefit of having done so living inside you.

That is **50 helps.**

But gang members are big, strong and tough and have boundless energy so let's say that instead of each of you helping just one person in a day you each help four people in a day in whatever good way you might be able to.

That is **200 helps.**

And now let's be ridiculous and say you can actually feel that the genuine help you gave to these people did something for you all individually, something inside you changed, you feel it even if you're not quite sure what it is and it has put this question into your mind.

How much better might I feel if I helped more people?

So you all decide that for one month you are each going to help four different people in your community every single day in whatever genuinely good way you can, for thirty days.

That is **6,000 helps.**

Do you think those **6,000 helps** would make a positive difference within your community?

Do you think people would regard you in a better way than they do now when you're causing so much fear and harm through your gang life?

Do you realise that if you gave those **6,000 helps** it wouldn't be long before doors started opening to you because people realised you're someone who was trying to make their lives and your life better?

No, it won't be easy, the road of good never is, dark energy sees it is so.

Evil is going to throw everything it can at you to tell you that what you are doing is nonsense, weakness and that the only road for you to follow is the one of alcohol, drugs, tobacco, bullying, lying, stealing and violence against other human beings.

That's the right road for you to follow?

That's the right thing for you to use the greatest gift in the universe for?

Really?

Who are you kidding?

Not me, because I see right through that kind of thinking.
It comes from your system training.

But then how about if, for an entire year, your 50 gang members each forced themselves to help four people every single day in a genuinely good way?

That would be **72,000 helps!**

And that's from one gang of just fifty members.

How about if **ten** similar gangs in a city all did the same thing?

That would be **720,000 helps** given to the wider community over a year.

Don't you think that would make an enormous difference for the better to the lives of everyone, whether they were giving or receiving those **helps?**

But doing this would mean following a road only really tough people are able to travel, the sort of people who have real inner strength and determination to make their own and everyone else's lives better.

Yes, that's a tough road for tough people.

But you're a gang member so that's you, isn't it?

Gang members are tough, aren't they?

Then how come this road of helping other people is too tough for you?

You mean you're not really that tough, you're only tough when you're living within the safety of the gang?

So in answer to **the question** 'In the moment my journey of life on earth is over what do I want to be able to say my life has been about?' you are going to say:

I never helped anyone but myself and the gang.

That's what I did with the greatest gift in the universe.

That's it?

That sums up your entire existence on earth?

That's what you want to be able to say you did while you were here?

Wow!

The gang is certainly stealing away all of the energy that belongs to you and keeping it for itself.

You can't change your life because that's just the way life is?

Because that's just the way things are?

I don't think so, I think your life is just the way you make it.

And it's up to you what you make your life into.

Try a day of helping people and see how it goes and what happens.

Then try another day and another day.

One thing is for sure.

You will have changed the road you're on.

No more fighting, wounding, maiming, killing, alcoholic and drug oblivion, police, fines, prison, hurt, hopelessness....

Not much of a prize worth fighting for, is it?

You are the Energy!

Don't Let The Energy Thieves Win!

<u>Knives, Guns, Weapons</u>

Always think of yourself as the centre of your energy and that out there in our world are countless cunning, devious and dangerous energy thieves determined to steal your energy so they can destroy your life. Most energy thieves have no energy, no life force and no power until you give them some of yours and then they'll steal it all!

I'll have a bet with you that if you were to put a gun on the table in front of you and stare at it for a million, billion, squillion, quadrillion, zillion, vermillion millennia that gun will not have wounded, maimed or killed anyone in all of that time, in fact it won't have done anything at all because it can't, it has no energy, no life force and no power.

You have all three.

Be absolutely sure about this:

When you manage the energy you have been given really badly and you make the mistake of reaching out to the gun:

It is your energy that picks it up.
It is your energy that aims it at another human being.
It is your energy that squeezes the trigger and makes the hammer fall onto the percussion cap.
It is your energy that explodes the charge in the cartridge.
It is your energy in the bullet that is fired down the barrel.
It is your energy that wounds, maims or kills another human being.

It is no one else's energy that does this, it is yours and yours alone.

It is not the gun that wounds, maims or kills because it cannot do anything by itself.

It is you who wounds, maims or kills!

Guns cannot kill people, people kill people and they use guns (and a heck of a lot of other things) to do it with.

If you don't reach out to the gun with the energy that you are it can never kill anyone.

Here is the most powerful reality of what is really going on when you reach out to a weapon:

When you reach out to the gun, the knife or a weapon of some kind then the moment your hand closes upon it – **it immediately controls all of the energy you are and it dictates how your life is going to be!**

It is the weapon that dictates to you how you will be!

The moment your hand closes around the weapon it runs your energy and your life – you don't anymore!

It feels as if you do, but that is the con of the energy thief.

The moment you let go of the weapon your energy comes back to you and you run your energy and your life once more and it does not!

If you hold or have a weapon on you sooner or later you are going to use it and in that moment of wounding, maiming or killing another human being the weapon will have damaged your life beyond repair.

If you hadn't had the weapon on you your life would have continued along a path where it was you who was managing the energy you have been given with the opportunity of guiding it down the road of good.

Instead the weapon has now dictated how your life and the life of the human being you used the weapon against will be from that moment onward.

The gun, the knife and all weapons are **dangerous to you** when they are in your possession because they are the most massive energy thieves who, in an instant, can change your life dramatically for the worse forever and drive the energy you are so far down into the dark void you can never, ever get back to where you were.

It says in an ancient and highly respected scripture:

Thou shalt not kill – and it says this for a very good reason.

Should you manage your energy so badly as to energise a gun and wound, maim or kill another human being two things will have happened in that instant.

First you will have damaged someone else's energy or you will have been the cause of their energy ceasing altogether.

In this respect you will have become the energy thief yourself and energy thieves in one way or another work for evil in its attempts to derail human energy from its true path, so now evil is in charge of your life and your energy, not you, and it has already sent you a long way down the dark road.

Second you will have lost a part of your own energy if you have damaged another human being's energy or ended it completely.

Your energy will never be the same afterwards, it can never be because it has been damaged forever, you have lost a part of it through using the gun and damaging or ending another human being's energy.

A piece of the energy you were created as, the greatest gift in the universe, will be gone forever and **you cannot get it back** no matter what you do or how hard you try!

It's not like getting your energy back from alcohol, drugs or tobacco.

We are talking about permanent, irreversible damage to the energy that you are.

People who have been trained to fight in militaries go to war and kill other human beings.

They come home changed by what they have done, no matter how much they don't appear to be or how much they try to hide it, their energy has been damaged and sooner or later they break down to a greater or lesser extent as that missing part of their energy begins to haunt them.

The system we live under actually trains people to think that when they wound, maim or kill other human beings they are doing the right thing, being strong and gaining in strength when in fact the very opposite is true.

Wounding, maiming or killing another human being means they have suffered massive damage to their energy.

These people have had their energy seriously damaged by their acts of killing, have lost huge amounts of energy and have been sidetracked down a dark road.

This is why they had to be trained and trained and trained and indoctrinated and indoctrinated and indoctrinated into believing they were in the right and that killing the enemy was the right thing to do with their energy until killing human beings became automatic to them and all thoughts about what they were really doing had been removed.

Otherwise they wouldn't have been killing human beings.

And it takes two sets of human beings on different 'sides' both having been trained and indoctrinated in this way to go to war, each believing that what they are doing is right.

As time passes after their acts of killing sooner or later remorse, another massive energy thief, kicks in and takes even more energy from them, often leading to depression, desolation and suicide.

Knives, guns, bullets and bombs are energy thieves!

If you reach out to them they will destroy your life and this is precisely what evil wants because it knows that whilst you are wounding, maiming and killing you are no longer in charge of the energy you are, it is.

The con of the energy thief is to get you to believe you are doing right and that you are in full control of your energy when nothing could be further from the truth.

It knows that whilst you are spinning around in the dark downward spiral it has trapped you in through your use of the weapon you can never find your true path or your true purpose because it has you travelling in the wrong direction.

Don't get me wrong, I'm not a pacifist, I believe in the absolute right of the individual human being to self defence. It's just that when you wound, maim or kill another human being you damage yourself so badly and that damage is permanent.

So how about we ban guns?

This is probably the most ineffective thing we can do because we fall straight into evil's trap.

Do I need to remind you about how devious evil is?

We banned drugs didn't we?

Fat lot of good that did us, drugs are prevalent in every section of society and can be bought as easy as buying your lunch.

After one of evil's henchmen, the dreadful energy thief Thomas Hamilton, murdered 16 school children and their teacher in Dunblane, Scotland on March 13th 1996 the UK government imposed a ban on handguns.

Handguns can still be bought illegally in the UK today.

Because once something is banned human beings want it!

It becomes exciting and daring to have it and it's seen as a test of manhood to break the law and not get caught, in other words to live dangerously.

This is evil working deviously on human energy.

It is not guns that need banning it is a change that each of us needs to make within ourselves so that we don't regard things that are banned as being somehow in some way or other beneficial to our lives and we recognise from a young age that precisely the opposite is true.

Clear thinking about guns will tell you they are energy thieves.

Poison is an energy thief, but you don't reach out to it and put it inside yourself, do you?

Guns are exactly the same, if you reach out and energise the gun you will maim, wound or kill someone, if you don't reach out to the gun you defeat evil and keep your energy for better use.

You simply have to get perspective on the fact that weapons are going to take your energy away from you as well as from the person you use them against.

Let's look at people who plant bombs and suicide bombers.

Most are driven by hatred, some by coercion, some by money and some through needing a cause.

That cause generates a feeling of security, of belonging to something, of doing something worthwhile. Those who are clever at manipulating the teaching and indoctrination of a human being can guide them to accept and follow any cause they want.

This is energy thievery of the worst kind and it's a heinous crime to commit against a fellow human being, the manipulation of someone else's energy to achieve your own aims.

Manipulating other people's energy can never be justified!

When manipulating someone to a warlike cause becomes easy evil will see to it that a life ends.

If someone is living in some kind of hell here on earth then it is relatively easy to turn their energy towards killing others with the promise of some great and fantastic reward, even if they have to kill themselves to get it.

If they won't consent then coercion through threatening members of their family can be used to make them comply.

Evil is swirling around them, about to steal all of their energy.

To get out of the miserable life they're in is the key to manipulating them and the less educated they are the easier they are to convince they should kill others and take their own life as well in order to receive that fantastic reward.

Hatred has to be fanned into flames within them and that hatred has first to be generated from somewhere by someone.

To take your own life in order to take the lives of others is the work of evil.

To shatter the gift you have received, to simply revoke it and throw it back at the giver along with shattering the gift that has been given to others and belongs to them, which you have no right to do, is a most appallingly dark act of pure evil.

Whatever reward the suicide bomber thinks they are going to receive it will certainly not be the realisation that their energy is going to belong to evil forever.

You see the true path for any human being to follow is the path of good, those who think their true path is to kill others as well as themselves walk the dark road even though they have been convinced through indoctrination and manipulation that the dreadful act they are going to commit is somehow gloriously good.

The con of the energy thief is dictating to them what they will do with their energy when they should be managing their energy themselves and directing it towards the cause of good and so finding their true path and living out their true purpose.

If you reach out to the weapon sooner or later it is guaranteed to ruin your existence – forever.

You are the Energy!

Don't Let The Energy Thieves Win!

Your Circumstances

Always think of yourself as the centre of your energy and that out there in our world are countless cunning, devious and dangerous energy thieves determined to steal your energy so they can destroy your life. Most energy thieves have no energy, no life force and no power until you give them some of yours and then they'll steal it all!

The system of life we live under wants you to believe that where you live and the environment that surrounds you is all there is and all there ever will be for you in this world and that's just how things are and that's just how your life's going to be.

It wants you to believe that you and your life are stuck where you are whether you like it or not and there is nothing whatsoever you can do about it.

This is nothing more than system nonsense and energy thievery on a massive scale.

Adolescents get stuck in a rut in their living environment and so rebel against it when they can no longer find anything new that holds interest or excitement for them.

They then turn to alcohol, drugs, tobacco, stealing, gangs, etc., anything to somehow try and change their lives and make their living environment more exciting and what they believe to be 'better'.

But by handing over their energy to these energy thieves all they are doing is allowing themselves to be robbed of their energy and led down a dark road that will stop them finding and following their true path to their true purpose.

There is only one real change they can make in order to help their lives and that is to change their living environment to a better one. This kind of move will give them the opportunity to change their lives for the better.

Always bear in mind that you only know what you know and that if the system has drummed into you that all you are going to know is that you have no option but to stay where you are and make the best of your life in a bad living environment then **it is lying to you.**

No one has commanded that you have to live on one particular spot on this earth for your entire existence.

No one has commanded that the energy you are has to be chained to one living environment.

No one has commanded that you dig that hole and sit in it waiting for the bomb to drop and the farthest you will ever travel is to the bottom of your garden.

No one has commanded that your life has to be the way it is forever.

The only person who ever thinks that these things are set in stone is you.

I know someone who was stuck in a rut and going nowhere, then one day they were bold enough to join the Navy and now they've grown into an amazing human being with an interesting life full of friends.

I met a couple of people working in a café in a top ski resort in Switzerland during the snow ski-ing season.
They were from Australia and had no money.
To earn a bit she gave massages and he taught ski-ing and they worked in the café, which entitled them to free ski passes for the entire season.

They could ski as much as they wanted in their spare time in an expensive resort for the entire season, yet they had no money.

They had changed their living environment and their lives by managing their energy cleverly enough to get themselves to the resort so they could ski.

Not only that but through their massages and ski instruction they were helping other people.

They could have sat on their hands in Australia and done nothing with their lives, but they decided to do something with their energy and they got a lot of enjoyment out of it.

If the system has tricked the energy you are to move towards becoming any of the following because you are bored with where you live and how life is for you then start working right now at changing your living environment and your direction in life and be very, very determined to make that change, because if you don't your time here is going to hurt you and give you more and more pain:

Alcoholic
Drug Addict
Drug Dealer
Tobacco Addict
Bully
Thief
Gambling Addict
Gang Member
Knife User
Gun User

You are not 'locked' into where your life on earth is situated, but the system will convince you that you are.

If where you are is a bad place, let's say it's some kind of ghetto, you absolutely must do whatever it takes to move yourself out of it, volunteer for everything you can especially to do some charity work that involves helping other people.

Doors will open to you if you do.

Your life can't be any worse living somewhere else doing something else and who knows, maybe it will become a whole lot better.

To keep learning everything you can about life so you keep expanding your comfort zone is crucial

You can learn by reading about the mistakes other people have made and then not making them yourself.

This will save you a lot of trouble, even through reading newspapers and determining that all the bad you see in them is not the life you want.

Then along will come something you will read, see or hear of that looks good and might be that chance for you to change.

Go for it, a door is opening, if it turns out not to be what you expected look for other doors that might be opening because of the move you tried to make.

If you are determined to change your circumstances then you will change them and you will make your life better.

Keep answering **the question** on page 8 twice every day and your answers will guide you.

Never think that your life has to be how it is and you cannot change it.

If your life is the way it is because of your circumstances, where you live and what is going on around you, then make a dramatic change that will give you the chance to make your life better.

Your life can become whatever you decide to direct your energy towards.

You are the Energy!

Don't Let The Energy Thieves Win!

Where's The Thief?

Always think of yourself as the centre of your energy and that out there in our world are countless cunning, devious and dangerous energy thieves determined to steal your energy so they can destroy your life. Most energy thieves have no energy, no life force and no power until you give them some of yours and then they'll steal it all!

This is another great question to keep asking yourself:

Where's the thief that is stealing my energy and knocking my life off course?

Your answers will expose who or what is stealing your energy and sapping you of it every day and keeping you from following your true path.

You need to think carefully about everything that is going on in your daily life and make a list of all those things you think might be acting as energy thieves against you.

Take your time and keep going back to the list and adding to it and when you're ready prioritise your list and put the biggest energy thieves, the ones that are doing you the most damage and that you need to take your energy back from and throw out of your life, right at the top.

Next you need to be determined that you are going to take full charge of your energy yourself and take it back from all of these energy thieves by working hard to remove them from your life one by one **until there are none left on the list!**

If you have the driving ambition that you want to get your energy back so that you have all of your energy once more to forge down the road of good and direct towards helping other people then you must work out a proper plan for dealing with the energy thieves that are robbing you of your life.

This may not be easy, but you are an imaginative, inventive and, if you want to be, unstoppable being. It may mean you have to make a complete life change (the energy thief fear will try to stop you doing this), or that you have to confront someone head on and perhaps end whatever relationship you have with them, or that you need to get them to grasp the fact that they are taking energy from you instead of enhancing your energy and they must stop doing so.

I recently got one unhappy person to think for a while about the energy thieves that might be operating against him and suddenly it hit him like a bolt from the blue. It was a family member who was acting as an energy thief by always wanting his help, wanting his money and wanting everything from him including tons of his time!

Once he had determined this he went straight home and laid down the law that this was to stop. Not that it was going to stop at some time in the future, but that it was stopped from that moment on and by doing this he was able to take his energy back and use it to change his life for the better.

He had to be very firm with this family member in order to take his energy back so he could use it to help others. But one result of his being firm was that the person who had been acting as an energy thief then began to change and deal with their own life in a much better way, so in the end they both won.

When the door closed on the person who was acting as an energy thief another door opened to them, another way for them to be and it helped them change the way they managed their energy for the better.

Whatever your way forward may be you need to use every ounce of your intelligence to work out the best way to manage your energy so you can rid yourself of anything that isn't contributing to it, anything that is not helping you grow stronger inside, making you calmer, more contented and helping to ensure you are following your true path.

If you are addicted to alcohol, drugs, tobacco, food or gambling you can take the war to these energy thieves because you now understand what they are really trying to do to you and you have proper perspective on them.

112

You can turn the tables on them by using **the weapon** and changing the way you manage your energy in order to beat them.

You can start making your life better immediately by asking yourself:

Where's the Thief?

So what happens when you begin knocking each energy thief that is stealing your energy and diverting you from your true path out of your life?

As the energy that was constantly leaving you returns does it all build up inside you and one day you go off bang?

Far from it, the first thing is that you suddenly find you have more time for yourself and then you may become tired as your body begins healing itself from all the stress and energy loss it was suffering, so give yourself a little recovery time, you can judge how much by how you are feeling.

Gradually you will find your immune system strengthens and you start feeling better and better and many different and positive perspectives about your life will come to you now that you are managing your energy in a better way.

And when you feel recovered from the ordeal the energy thieves were putting you through all you have to do is channel your energy in a direction that will guarantee your life will become more fulfilling and rewarding than you would ever have believed.

The greatest calling for the human spirit
is to turn selflessly
and help another human being!

You are the Energy!

Don't Let The Energy Thieves Win!

The Garden of Energy Thieves

Always think of yourself as the centre of your energy and that out there in our world are countless cunning, devious and dangerous energy thieves determined to steal your energy so they can destroy your life. Most energy thieves have no energy, no life force and no power until you give them some of yours and then they'll steal it all!

When you first arrive here on earth the system we live under grabs you and begins to train and indoctrinate the energy you are so it can bind your energy to itself.

As you set up your comfort zone your teachers are your parents, your siblings, those around you at playschool and those who look after you there.

You believe everything you are told and everything you are taught because you know no different. You have not yet experienced the results of being lied to so it is easy for the system to lead you down whichever road it chooses right from the very beginning.

No one warns you about the energy thieves and the fact that you have been created as the energy they will constantly try to take away from you.

No one tells you about the never ending war between good and evil that rages around you every second of your existence as they fight over the energy that belongs to you.

No one teaches you that you have inbuilt powerful weaponry to use to protect yourself from evil and beat all of its energy thieves.

No one tells you that you have powerful inner attributes that can lead you to a better existence if you would only access and use them to help you find your true path.

You are simply left to the ravages of the system we live under as it indoctrinates you into believing everything it tells you is true, the right way for you to live, the right way for you to be.

Like most human beings you need to find a cause to follow to help enhance your comfort zone and give you a feeling of 'security of purpose'. You give your energy to causes you think are right because the system has trained you how and what to think, when many of these causes help no one, including you.

A cause can swiftly gain power over your energy and consequently you may allow hatred and anger to flourish within you, for example you may further the activities of a gang, carry weapons with which to harm others and, even worse, misuse the energy you have been given by encouraging others to do the same.

Living this way means you are only furthering the power of the system over the energy that has been given to you and to humanity.

You have no idea, no conception at all that it is evil which has deviously managed to get itself into control of the energy that you are because no one ever explained to you how this could happen.

You are never able to clearly see what is really going on when it comes to looking at your life or realise you have the option of beating off evil's attacks upon your energy so that you can change the road you're on and make your life a whole lot better.

You live out your existence in a twilight world simply trying to survive along with the bulk of humanity, never wondering if you could lead a higher, better and more wonderful existence of enormous benefit to yourself and to others.

The system we live under has made sure of everything you will know and everything you will never know.

You only know what you know....

And what you don't know is vast....

And everything you know has been taught to you by the system and you operate your existence within the limits of this knowledge and cling to the confines of it for safety.

It is the same for each of us.

So if your parents and those who taught you didn't know about the energy thieves and the improvement in life that can be gained through beating them by using good energy management, because they themselves were unwitting indoctrinated products of the system, then you will be too.

It is that kind of teaching and limitation of your knowledge the system depends on because it is that limitation of knowledge you will operate your energy and your life within and in this way the system is able to control your energy for its own ends.

It seems as if everything the system teaches you to direct your energy towards is the right way to live your life, the right way for you to be.

But is it?

Who convinced you that giving your energy to alcohol, drugs and tobacco, or being a gang member and using a knife or a gun against your fellow human beings was the right way to be?

The system, that's who, this is what it taught you and got you to accept as being 'normal' and so you simply surrendered the great gift of your energy to one or more of its energy thieves in the belief that this was the right way to live your life.

Having the energy you are taught, trained and indoctrinated in this way means your life can easily follow a dark road without you even realising you're on it or where you're heading and you may never know the existence of any other road.

If this is happening to you then the system's work of teaching you how and what to think, how to react to events and how you should be is complete and in this way it will own the energy that was given to you forever.

Through developing a broader knowledge of life and achieving perspective on what could be a better way for you to exist, such as ridding yourself of the energy thieves, you could quickly change your management of the energy that you are in the most beneficial of ways and so begin ensuring you make the most of your tiny fragment of time here.

When you came to the earth you didn't know it and no one told you, but you entered the Garden of Energy Thieves.

They are here to test the way you manage your energy and they will do you just as much harm as they can, or as little as you allow them to.

You need to work out which of them is stealing your energy, which of them is damaging you and diverting you from your true path and begin removing them from your life by managing the energy you are differently to the way you have in the past.

You first have to cast off and throw aside your training and indoctrination by the system we live under so you can get back to being the real you.

Your self-honesty will play a big part in this.

Once you have pushed aside your system trained beliefs about the right way to be then you can work on guiding the energy that was given to you away from the energy thieves down a much better path, your true path.

You do not do this for recognition by others or for some fantastic reward, you do this for you, so that you can take pride, contentment, comfort and fulfilment from having carried out the mission you have been charged with:

To manage the greatest gift in the universe, the energy that has been given to you, in the best possible way that you can while you are here.

And then one day, hopefully a long way in the future, in the moment your experience of life here on earth is over you will be able to hold your head high and proudly declare to yourself that this was what you did with the greatest gift in the universe whilst you were upon the earth.

You did not waste the gift, not for a single second.

You are the Energy!

Don't Let The Energy Thieves Win!

<u>Managing Your Energy</u>

1/. The Guardian:

You are the guardian of the greatest gift in the universe, the energy you have been created as.

The energy, life force and power you have received are yours to manage in the best possible way that you can whilst you are here.

**Unless you believe in reincarnation
your life is not a dress rehearsal!**

2/. Honesty:

Be totally honest with yourself at all times and give good, honest guidance to your energy and your life so you can follow your true path and live out your true purpose.

3/. The Question:

Be sure to ask yourself **the question** twice every day looking into a mirror in complete honesty with yourself:

**In the moment my journey of life on earth is over
what do I want to be able to say my life has been about?**

4/. **Good:**

Watch for the way that good works mysteriously in life and treasure and appreciate it when you see it happening.

You may find that good does not always **appear** to be your friend who is here to help you or make you feel better because, unlike evil, it is not trying to trick you out of your energy. All you have to do is have faith in yourself and keep following the path of good and you will feel good accompanying you as you reap the life changing benefits that doing so will bring you.

5/. **The Energy Thieves:**

The energy thieves will try to take your energy away from you, knock you from your true path and divert your energy down endless, downward spiralling dark roads so that you cannot find your true path and purpose while you are here.

An energy thief will not take just a little of your energy, if you give it the chance it will take all of your energy away from you and leave you with none!

6/. **Be Alert:**

Be forever alert and watchful for the attacks of the energy thieves and remember to think about how deviously they might be working to steal your energy and your life away from you so you can expose them for what they really are.

Whenever you're feeling down, whenever you're hurting or someone is annoying or bullying you, whenever you feel yourself getting out of control through alcohol or drugs or whenever you go to pick up a weapon:

THINK THIEF!

7/. **Evil:**

Be constantly aware that evil is working deviously against you and guard yourself by identifying it, achieving perspective on it and guiding your energy away from it towards the Light.

Evil will try to con you into thinking it is your friend, that it is here to help you and make you feel better when all the time its sole intention is to steal your energy, damage you as much as possible and get the energy that you are 'off planet' as soon as it can.

So keep a thorough, constant and watchful eye out for evil and how it might be working against you.

8/. **Where's The Thief?**

Always ask yourself **'where's the thief?'** throughout your life.

Once you have identified each thief that is stealing your energy and knocking your life off course you can change the way you manage your energy in order to beat the thief.

9/. **The Weapon:**

Use **the weapon** of instantly directing your energy away from every energy thief that crosses your path.

Recognise the thief!

Remember what to do!

Activate the weapon!

Go help someone!

10/. **You Only Know What You Know:**

Accept that **you only know what you know** and you operate your energy within what you know and that what you know has been taught to you by the system we live under for the purpose of binding the energy that was given to you to itself forever.

Keep your eyes, your mind and your heart open to learning and being receptive to new ideas and take every possible opportunity to increase your knowledge of all things, especially life, at all times.

11/. **Help Others:**

To dramatically improve both your energy and your life start helping other people and never stop helping them, then watch for the doors that will begin opening to you and boldly walk through them to change the road you're on and you will be following your true path on the way to finding your true purpose.

Help yourself through helping others

Here are two questions you can ask yourself:

> **How many people am I going to help today?**
> At the beginning of the day make your target.
>
> At the end of the day:
> **How many people have I helped today?**

12/. **Use The Tools:**

Train yourself into giving good management and guidance to your energy at all times by using everything you have learned and all the tools in the message within this book because they are here to help you.

50 Ways To Help Someone

Give them a smile

Give them a hug

Say something cheery

Be friendly

Make someone laugh

Listen to what they have to say and continue the conversation, you may be the only person they have to talk to

Offer them your help to do anything they need doing

Go and do their shopping for them

Take them shopping

Show them where to shop cheaply

Take them to the hospital

Take them to the doctor

Take them to the dentist

Take them to see their favourite sports match live

Invite someone round to see their favourite sport's big occasion on your widescreen TV

Take someone for a walk on a beach or by a river

Take someone for a round of golf

Visit people in hospital and cheer them up

Wash someone's dishes

Wash someone's car and valet the inside

If you're a mechanic fix their car for them for free

Clean their kitchen

Clean their house

Clean their yard

Paint their house

Paint their fence

Paint their gates

Look after their kids while they take a rest

Look after their pets while they take a rest

Phone someone you should have a long time ago, they might not be here tomorrow and they'll appreciate your call

Write a letter to someone you should have a long time ago

Email someone you should have a long time ago

Go and see that old lady who lives alone down the street, offer her your help and be some company for her, don't let her be lonely

Write a cheque and send it to a charity

Volunteer to help a charity

Volunteer to work in your local soup kitchen for the homeless

Bake something, cook some food and take it to those less fortunate than you

Invite someone to lunch or dinner if you think they're in need of a good meal or some company

Hold a jumble sale or garage sale of all your old stuff and give the money to a local good cause

Give your old clothes to those less fortunate than you

When someone's life ends don't hang back, get stuck in and be a comforting presence, being around can ease the situation

Help someone lose weight by losing weight with them

Show someone your appreciation of who they are

Show someone your appreciation of what they do

Share your car when you drive to work

Share your car if you're going to drive a long journey, be ingenious and find people to share the whole journey or a part of it

Take someone for a holiday or a short break they would never be able to take on their own

Ask someone how they're doing and tell them you think they're doing really well

If someone says they're doing badly or having a hard time, be their friend, listen to their troubles, give the best advice you can

Don't let someone be alone if you think they are a danger to themselves, if they might need professional help get it to them without hesitation

Many people are worse off than you and are having a seriously bad time.

You have the power through the way you manage your energy to help them make their lives better.

By doing this you will change the road you are on and make your own life better, but it is only you who can make this change and you only have this tiny fragment of time in which to do your best to get it right!

So Now It's Up To You!

Good Luck to You, My Friend!

The Clock of Life is Ticking Its Way Through Your Tiny Fragment of Time!

Be Bold!

Follow Your True Path!

Don't Just Sit There!

Go Help Someone!

You are the Energy!

Do not let the Energy Thieves take it away from you!

A great way for you to help people is to tell them about my books and websites, then you'll be helping me help them, so you'll be helping them!

My books are available at: www.EnergyThieves.com

You can also get your **free 'Friend of Jess' Certificate** to print out and frame there!

When people see your Certificate they will ask how you got it, this gives you the opportunity to spread the word about the message of help in this book and how it helped you or perhaps someone you know - then once again you will be helping others.

You can also print out **free Certificates**
for your family and friends as gifts!

I will be releasing a number of **help videos** on the subjects in my books at some stage on the following website:

www.BeatingTheEnergyThieves.com

To keep in touch and receive news updates, details of future book and video releases and much more please be sure to leave your contact details at EnergyThieves.com.

Find out about Books 2, 3 & 4 on the following pages!

How to Beat the Energy Thieves® *And Make Your Life Better* - **Book 2:** How to Stop Emotions, Food, People, Problems and Traumas Damaging Your Energy And Your Life, So You Can Live Out Your True Purpose And Be Happy.

How you can stop your energy being held hostage by all kinds of emotions including fear, anger, loneliness, hatred, stress and many more, so they cannot dictate your life to you.

How to deal with big event nerves such as exam or public speaking nerves.

How it is you who turns food into an energy thief if you don't stick to the closely guarded ancient secret 'Formula for Life'!

How to cope with major problems and what you can do to help yourself when you're stuck right in the middle of one.

How to cope with financial wipe out and everything you can do to help yourself get through this dreadful situation (as I have).

How the people around you can be stealing your energy and knocking your life off course without you even realising it and what you can do to stop this happening.

How you can defeat the traumas you have suffered in your life, the things that live in your past and hurt you in the present, and stop them from constantly stealing your energy.

How to win and what being a winner really is, not the version the system wants you to believe, and why you should always strive to be a winner in this way.

Why you should never think you have been wasting your life up until the moment you heard a part of this message that resonated with you.

Because you definitely have not!

And another 50 ways to help someone!

Energy 3 will be published in first quarter 2012

How to Beat the Energy Thieves® *And Make Your Life Better* – **Book 3:** How Education, Indoctrination, The Media, Technology, Role Models, Gossip, Trivia, Self Importance and Arrogance Can Ruin Your Life.

How everything your teachers and the system we live under teach you may or may not be the right way for you to live your life.

How your training and indoctrination by the system we live under enables it to control the energy that belongs to you.

How the media influences your thinking and opinions about everyday matters and consequently you use this limited knowledge about life instead of having the broadest possible base of knowledge to work with so you can live a better, more informed life.

How technology can become a major energy thief unless you use it only for what you absolutely need.

How role models can dramatically affect the direction of your life and how you are a constant role model for other people without realising it.

How idle gossip can ruin your life and the lives of others, which is why you shouldn't involve yourself in idle gossip.

How the trivia of life can bog down your energy and make you go round and round in circles getting more and more unhappy because you don't seem to be getting anywhere.

How self importance and arrogance can take charge of your energy and create false beliefs in your mind about yourself to ensure that your life lacks love, warmth and real friendships and consequently becomes more and more miserable.

Also providing you with a list of your life's 'friends and enemies', how many of these enemies can you get rid of from your life?

Book 4 is coming in third quarter 2012 - please see next page

129

Books 1 to 3 give you information about Energy Thieves and how they can damage your life and **Book 4** will top them!

Here are just a few of the subjects that Book 4 will deal with:

Money
Possessions
War
Criminality
Government
Power
Control
Poverty
Starvation
Belief Systems
Division...............and much, much more!

There are massive Energy Thieves out there in our world and Book 4 looks at how they steal and manipulate your energy without caring about you in the slightest or what you can do about them.

Perspective concerning these giant Energy Thieves is crucial because it means you will be able to benefit through guiding your energy in a better way as you use this increased knowledge about life.

Blending the information in Books 1 to 4 into your life mix will help you achieve huge perspective over your energy and the things that can take it away from you so easily and make your life hurt.

If one reader of my books out of 100 takes the hurt out of their lives by beating the Energy Thieves that will be something special.

If one reader in 10 takes the hurt out of their lives by beating the Energy Thieves that will be something remarkable.

And if you can beat all the Energy Thieves that are responsible for hurting your life, then that will be something truly epic.

Book 4 will be published in third quarter 2012

Please register your details at EnergyThieves.com

www.ingramcontent.com/pod-product-compliance
Lightning Source LLC
Chambersburg PA
CBHW061733020426
42331CB00006B/1232